THE CIRCLE OF
LEADERSHIP

THE CIRCLE OF LEADERSHIP

A FRAMEWORK FOR CREATING & LEVERAGING CULTURE

ANDREW ADENIYI

NEW DEGREE PRESS

COPYRIGHT © 2020 ANDREW ADENIYI

THE CIRCLE OF LEADERSHIP

A Framework for Creating & Leveraging Culture

ISBN   978-1-64137-908-3   *Paperback*

          978-1-64137-647-1   *Kindle Ebook*

          978-1-64137-649-5   *Ebook*

CONTENTS

THE CIRCLE OF LEADERSHIP FRAMEWORK

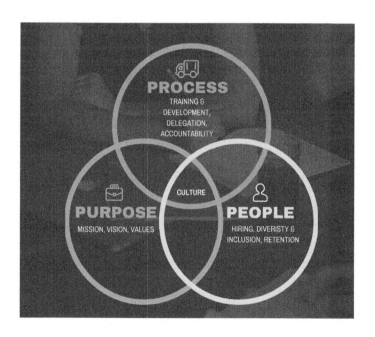

INTRODUCTION: THE CIRCLE OF LEADERSHIP

"Culture eats strategy for breakfast."

−PETER DRUCKER

***

EXCEEDING EXPECTATIONS

I learned about the opportunity of a lifetime in the summer of 2017. I was a district manager for an international grocery chain and a top performer in their Central Indiana (CI) division. CI was widely considered a top-three division out of over twenty divisions in its US operations. It would be an understatement to say I was extremely ambitious and hungry for a larger role with more influence. During my first three-plus years with the organization, I had led several projects in addition to leading a district of stores to consistently high performance. My reputation for achieving results and influencing people allowed me to be considered a leader amongst my peers, which got me exactly what I was asking for.

At the time, I was one of eight district managers selected across the country to assist in the renovation of existing stores, as well as building new stores in their struggling Washington, DC (DC) division. It was an honor and a privilege to accept this role and the increased level of responsibility that came with it. Although I was slightly concerned about what to expect during my transition to the DC division, I went into the situation with an open mind and hoped for the best. It did not take long for me to realize why the DC division I was temporarily transferred to was considered one of the worst divisions in the company.

PRESIDENTIAL PREP

As my weekly conversation with my leader from the DC division was coming to an end, I started to second guess if the president of the company was really coming to the division the following week. I had heard through the grapevine that he was coming, but I needed to hear it from my leader to confirm. Right before we got off the phone, my leader finally addressed what was on my mind and said, "Hey, Andrew, you might have heard already, but the president of the company will be in the division next week."

Trying to act surprised, I quickly responded, "Really? Do you know what stores he will be visiting?" She then proceeded to tell me that he would be visiting a store in Northern Virginia that was covered by one of my peers. What she said next would change everything on my calendar for the next week.

"Yes," she answered. "Although he will not be in your market, we need you to cover for Abby's stores since she will be on vacation." I quickly realized that it would be a long week. Preparing for a presidential visit was no small task, regardless of which division you were in. There was a universal expectation of ensuring product quality was up to standard, signage and cleanliness were as close to perfect as possible, and that the store was 100 percent up to date with planograms and layouts. However, the difference between the CI and DC divisions centered around the expectation of how that preparation was executed.

In CI, I was not expected to invest a significant amount of labor hours in preparing for a presidential visit. The goal was to get the store in excellent shape within the flow of normal operations. In DC, I was expected to invest as many hours as it took to get the store perfect even though that was an unrealistic expectation. A store could never be perfect regardless of how many hours you invested in it. I also disagreed with the approach of trying to get the store perfect because it was an unrealistic depiction of store operations. If I were president, I would want to know what conditions my customers dealt with on a daily basis instead of getting a false image of excellence.

Unfortunately, it was not my place to decide on how to prepare my peer's store for the visit. So, I took the orders I was given and executed them to the best of my ability. The visit went extremely well after I worked sixteen-hour days for almost a week straight to prepare and an overnight shift the day before the president arrived. Although it was a significant investment of my time as well as my employees' time, the store looked great for the visit. However, I would learn an extremely stressful workweek was just the beginning.

LACK OF APPRECIATION

The true problem with the situation was that my director never acknowledged the work my team and I put in to preparing the store for the visit. In fact, I never received a simple "thank you" for filling in for my vacation partner. This situation would have never occurred in the CI division. Not only would I have not been expected to work overnight to prepare or work as many hours as I did, but I can also guarantee my director and the vice president of my division would have given me recognition for my efforts.

As I tried not to judge my new division too quickly, I was constantly reminded that I was not in CI anymore. The caliber of leadership I experienced in the DC division led to poor employee engagement, low productivity, and higher turnover than I had experienced in the CI division. I tried to keep an open mind, but that continued to be a tall task, as poor management became the rule rather than the exception in DC. I witnessed several distinct differences between the CI and DC divisions. Here are some of my key observations in DC:

- Lack of trust amongst the team
- Lack of professionalism
- Little to no empathy
- Lack of empowerment

- Poor culture
- Minimal senior leadership engagement

After a few months into my project role in the DC division, I was able to pick up on all of those issues. Ultimately, the root cause of their poor performance stemmed from poor leadership and poor culture. In the CI division, it was the complete opposite. We took pride in being the best. We competed against ourselves. We set the standard and then tried to exceed it. In DC, they accepted lackluster performance. Before we can discuss how to cultivate culture, we need to figure out who should be held accountable for creating it.

CULTIVATING CULTURE

Whose responsibility is it to create and reinforce culture? The answer is senior leadership. Leadership has the ability to influence behavior. When behavior is influenced consistently over time, culture starts to form. If it's a good culture, employee engagement will most likely be high. Every organization has a culture; the question is whether it is an effective culture or not.

The CI division had a leader who positively influenced the culture every day. The DC division had a leader who also influenced culture but in a negative way. He was a leader who led out of fear, which the worst leaders often do. He did not take time to personally connect with his team. You'd think that after transferring from across the country to assist his division, he would know basics about me, such as how long I had been in the division or what area of the division I was working in. This could not be further from the truth.

Almost six months into my time in DC, I had a brief conversation with the vice president of the DC division. He had no clue where my market of stores were or how long I had been in his division. This was a huge turnoff for me and made me feel like he did not really care or value my contributions to his division. This type of behavior led to a lack of trust between him and the rest of the people in the division, me included. Lack of effective culture and leadership is the reason why people in the DC division were so complacent and did not strive for greatness.

What kind of impact does leadership and culture have on performance? Great question. Although numbers may not tell the entire story, they certainly do not lie. I was shocked at what the numbers revealed.

RETURN ON CULTURE (NUMBERS DON'T LIE)

"Ninety-four percent of executives and 88 percent of employees believe a distinct workplace culture is important to business success."[1] However, despite the significant amount of research that shows there are culture issues in organizations across America, leaders and companies fail to make the right changes to improve. Lack of awareness and knowledge are not the majority of the reasons either. As you take a closer look, you will continue to find that there is a gap between what is known and what is actually done about the issue.

---

1   "Company Culture and Employee Engagement Statistics," CultureIQ, March 19, 2019.

According to Deloitte, "Only 12 percent of executives believe their companies are driving the 'right culture.'"[2] So, what you have is a clear understanding that a problem exists but a lack of effort and know-how allocated toward driving the culture in the right direction. This is one of my motivating drivers for writing this book. Even in situations where effort is put forth, the intangibles like communication, culture, and purpose are usually not the benefactors of those initiatives.

Leveraging intangibles such as culture is not only the right thing to do, it also makes perfect business sense to do so. When you look at peer sales numbers, you also find that "Companies with strong cultures saw a four times increase in revenue growth."[3] Continued focus on leading by example, hiring effectively, and aligning everyone toward a common mission can lead to an excellent work environment. The statistics show that very clearly.

Over 80 percent of people believe that you can gain a competitive advantage through your workplace culture.[4] And ultimately, it falls on leadership to enhance their organization's culture. One of the issues with organizational culture is the leadership team may struggle to fully understand and articulate their organization's culture. "Fewer than one in three executives (28 percent) report that they understand their organization's culture. They know culture is

---

2   Graham Little, "Deloitte Human Capital Trends in Perspective: The Science of Organization Design and Operation," (2017).
3   "Company Culture and Employee Engagement Statistics."
4   "Shape Culture," Deloitte Insights, Accessed June 3, 2020.

important but don't understand it."[5] We must hold leaders accountable.

If your culture is ineffective and unattractive, look at the leader. "Seventy percent of the variance between lousy, good, and great cultures can be found in the knowledge, skills, and talent of the team leader."[6] Once leadership can conquer the challenging yet rewarding task of creating or enhancing culture, your team will eventually be happier and more engaged.

Too many leaders try to increase productivity by focusing on training curriculum, bonuses that don't positively influence long-term behavior, and other tangible items when simply making them happier will make them more productive and more engaged. Making your employees happy can increase their productivity by 12 percent.[7] When I asked the CEO of Trek10, Shane Fimbel, what advice he would give to entrepreneurs and leaders, he said, "Do whatever you think will make you happy." As the leader of a rapidly growing tech company based out of South Bend, Indiana, he realized "If you go to a place where you're happy, you're going to do great work."

With such a glaring issue facing organizations, it made me ask the question "why?" Why do we continue to see significant issues with leadership and culture? Why are so many employees not engaged at work? What I discovered would

5   Graham Little, "Deloitte Human Capital Trends in Perspective: The Science of Organization Design and Operation."

6   Jim Clifton, "Are You Sure You Have a Great Workplace Culture?" May 5, 2020.

7   Claire P. Dodson, "Why Happy Employees Are 12% More Productive," Fast Company, July 31, 2015.

change the way I understood what I considered the tangibles and intangibles of business. It's all in the details.

INTANGIBLE LEADERSHIP

I believe that if business leaders focused more on the intangibles rather than the tangible aspects of leadership, leaders would find themselves more effective.

Leaders who understand the value in focusing on the intangibles such as employee engagement, purpose, communication, and accountability will create organizational cultures that can serve as a competitive advantage. Unfortunately, "Only 46 percent of companies report that they're prepared to tackle the engagement challenge."[8] Given the consistent mediocre satisfaction and engagement statistics that are released each year, this is problematic. And to make matters worse, "Nearly one in five employees (18 percent) reported that their companies don't formally measure employee engagement at all."[9] So how big of a problem is employee engagement really when we consider all factors?

In order to tackle this Goliath of a problem that organizations across the United States are facing, I have constructed a model that will help both current and aspiring leaders and

---

8 Graham Little, "Deloitte Human Capital Trends in Perspective."
9 Ibid.

entrepreneurs to better create and leverage culture in their organizations. It does not matter if you lead a committee at church; a non-profit, private, or public company; or a big or small business—this book is for you.

My mentality of "how can I learn more" equipped me with the knowledge, passion, and confidence to tackle leadership and culture. The truth of the matter is we should all be continuous learners and strive to maintain a high level of curiosity—especially for subjects that interest us. If you're wondering what differentiates me and my perspective from other thought-leaders and authors, keep reading.

WHY ME?

If one of the largest international grocery chains struggled to pinpoint how to enhance culture and leadership in certain divisions, then certainly there are other organizations struggling with the same thing. This thought was one of many that propelled me into the journey of writing on leadership and organizational culture. After experiencing leadership and culture in several organizations including public, privately owned, non-profits, international organizations, and more, I feel compelled and highly qualified to speak on this subject. I have my 10,000 hours in.

As a first-generation Nigerian-American with almost ten years of executive leadership experience, a bachelor's degree in Entrepreneurship and Corporate Innovation from Indiana University Bloomington, and a master's degree in Management, Strategy, and Leadership from Michigan State University, I believe I have a unique perspective on leadership and culture. I am the co-founder of a diversity, equity, and inclusion non-profit called CAN I BE REAL Inc. that was established in 2019. I also am the founder and CEO of AAA Solutions LLC. where I provide coaching and consulting services to small business owners.

The process of writing this book has afforded me the opportunity to discover new insights and expand on my knowledge. Through hundreds of interviews, books, articles, podcast episodes, and more, I have strengthened my knowledge in the field of culture, entrepreneurship, and leadership.

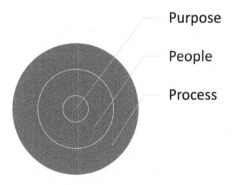

Purpose

People

Process

THE CIRCLE OF LEADERSHIP

The Circle of Leadership is an entrepreneurial framework on how to win by creating and leveraging culture. This book explores how intangible leadership can help you experience success by focusing on things that can be difficult to measure. This book is for those who are in a position of influence, for leaders who want to grow, and for people bold enough to challenge the status quo. For those willing to strive to exceed expectations and become the best version of themselves, this book was created for you.

This book will help you avoid the pitfalls that thousands of organizations struggle with. These pitfalls are similar to the issues that were commonplace in the DC division. I will highlight best practices from companies such as Southwest Airlines, Google, Intel, and Disney, as well as key findings from thought leaders such as Brené Brown, Simon Sinek, Patrick Lencioni, Jim Collins, and more. At the conclusion of this book, you will not only be equipped with knowledge of the importance of culture and leadership but also how to leverage culture to win in your organization. Implementing this model will help you improve the culture of your organization, which will lead to above-average performance.

The Circle of Leadership is a framework I first heard about early in my career from a former employer. However, I always felt like the model was missing some key parts. In my version, the framework begins with asking the question "why?" The first step in the process is to understand your purpose by asking "why?" as many times as possible. In order for employees to be engaged, they first need a compelling purpose. A mission, vision, and compelling set of core values can provide this. This step is crucial as it serves as the foundation of the entire model and helps determine what type of culture your organization will have.

The next phase in the model is to hire the right people who can help accomplish the mission—starting with senior leadership. Leaders influence everything in the organization, so it is important to have the right people calling the shots. As more people join the organization, it becomes even more important to take your time to hire the right person while creating a diverse and inclusive place to work. This book will dissect what this process should entail.

Once the foundation for culture is laid, there is a unified purpose. With the right people on the team in the right roles, the model will help leaders learn how to train, develop, and retain top talent. It does not matter how good a team member is if you cannot get them to stay with your organization and be engaged. This stage of the framework will cover everything from appreciation, recognition, and performance management.

Moreover, this book will cover the proper way to test the comprehension of your team once they have been trained effectively and empowered to accomplish tasks. You cannot delegate tasks and responsibilities to team members without being clear in expectations and following up with them to ensure they understand why their job matters and what success looks like in their role. This book will talk about how to build trust with your team and create an engaged, customer-centric, and empowered organization.

Lastly, the book will demonstrate how to create a culture of accountability within your organization. By instilling an expectation of team members taking extreme ownership within their realm of responsibility, you will be positioning your organization to achieve optimal health. Winning organizations encourage a culture of communication and feedback. The content toward the end of the book will help leaders determine how to do this effectively. Each chapter will conclude with a set of activity questions designed to help you apply the content. Once you absorb the content, it is up to you to implement it!

The Circle of Leadership is the perfect intersection of research, story-telling, and practical application to help you win as a leader.

Enjoy.

CHAPTER 1:

CULTIVATING CULTURE

"Culture is the unwritten, yet commonly shared set of beliefs that guide behavior."

—ANDREW ADENIYI

***

THE $6,000 EGG

Losing $6,000 over an egg is something that would make most business leaders cringe. However, failures like this happen more often than you would think. The financial impact of poor leadership can be catastrophic.

In episode #132 of *The Entreleadership Podcast,* author and entrepreneur Todd Duncan explained the story of *The $6,000 Egg.* As frequent visitors of a local restaurant in Newport Beach, California, it's safe to say that Todd and his wife Deb enjoyed their experience at this particular restaurant. According to Todd, "We were probably spending—between business events and our personal events—about 500 bucks a month at this restaurant."[10] However, all that would change as a result of one less than satisfactory experience.

One weekend, Todd and Deb grabbed lunch at this particular Newport Beach restaurant and decided they wanted to indulge in a cheeseburger. Todd and his wife had eaten the cheeseburger in the past and figured they would help themselves to it again, as a reward for exercising earlier in the day. To make the meal even more decadent, they decided to order an egg to go on top of the cheeseburger. Since the waiter had previously mentioned that the special for the day included a sunny-side-up egg, Todd and Deb figured this would be an easy addition to their burger.

Before the server could confirm the request, she informed Todd and Deb that she would have to check with the kitchen to verify they could accommodate the special request. The server soon returned only to inform them that the kitchen could not add the egg. Her explanation was "They are too busy."[11] Surprised by the response, especially since the special for the day included eggs and waffles, Todd tried to order the modified cheeseburger with another server they knew well.

However, the second server had a similar response. He said he needed to check with the kitchen to see if they could do it. Upon return, he stated, "They are too busy and aren't prepared to do anything that isn't on the menu."[12] At this

---

10   Coleman, Ken. "#132: Todd Duncan—The New Rules of Customer Service". Podcast. The Entreleadership Podcast, 2016.
11   Ibid.
12   Ibid.

point, Todd requested to speak to the manager to seek further clarification. As the manager, Natalie, arrived at their table, Todd could tell by her body language and facial expression that she was not going to be friendly. Natalie's first words to the couple were "So I understand you have a problem?"[13]

Todd went on to explain how they wanted a side order of an egg and Natalie quickly responded by telling the couple that they order a specific number of eggs per day and with the special for the day including eggs, they could not deviate from their menu items or else they would run out of eggs for their popular dish. After Natalie confirmed that they could not accommodate the egg request, Todd clarified the magnitude of her decision.

"So, let me make sure we are tracking here. I spend at least $6,000 a year at your restaurant, and I have one simple request for a two-dollar egg for my burger. You are telling me you can't make that happen because you only order enough eggs for your waffle dish?" Natalie responded with a firm "Yes," and Todd proceeded to ask her, "As a manager, wouldn't you rather be one egg short and throw away a waffle that probably costs you fifty cents to make than throw away a loyal customer who brings you $6,000 a year?"

She said, "It's our policy."[14]

---

13   Ibid.
14   Ibid.

Safe to say that Todd and his wife left the restaurant as disgruntled customers and perplexed by the fact that the restaurant—or at least the management—did not understand how to take care of customers. Instead of sending an employee to a nearby grocery store to buy a few cartons of eggs for less than $10, the manager allowed customers to walk away upset and miss out on $6,000 over the span of twelve months. What made the situation even worse was Natalie said, "I'm happy to take care of your bill for your inconvenience."[15] Not only were Natalie and the establishment willing to upset regular customers by not fulfilling their simple request, but they were also willing to lose even more money over an egg.

Let's peel back the onion a little bit to figure out why a leader would ever put their organization in this type of position.

---

15   Ibid.

PEOPLE OVER POLICY

This restaurant failed to prioritize people over policy. If the manager fostered a culture of doing the right thing vs. following policies, the servers may have acted differently. This isn't to say that policies are not important because they are. However, the ultimate responsibility should be on customer satisfaction. Todd went on to explain how companies need to adopt a philosophy of not saying no to customers.

A customer-centric, empowered culture is what companies should strive to foster. When team members are empowered to make decisions and rarely feel the need to ask management for approval, you have an empowered culture.

Whole Foods is an example of an empowered culture. In fact, they believe so much in the principle of saying yes to customers whenever possible that they decided to carry Todd's book in their stores.

To create a culture of saying yes, you must have competent leadership that understands the value of the customer. You then need those leaders to model the behavior they are trying to embed in the culture while training team members on how to satisfy customers. Engaging with customers and connecting with them emotionally can have a direct effect on your financials. In Todd's interview with *The Entreleadership Podcast*, he referenced a few statistics from Gallup that showed "emotional connection increases margins by as much as 26 percent" and you can impact sales by as high as 86 percent.[16] If serving customers to your utmost ability wasn't enough motivation in itself, hopefully, the numbers behind doing so will get more leaders to get their teams to emotionally engage with customers.

LEAD BY EXAMPLE

I've personally witnessed the impact of leaders cultivating a culture of trust, empowerment, and customer service. One of my former store managers named Randy did an excellent job of connecting with customers. Randy could often be seen carrying items from the store to a customer's trunk or walking a customer to every item on their shopping list. "I want my customers to feel highly satisfied with their shopping experience every time they come into my store, and to ensure that, I make sure my team knows the importance of excellent customer service," Randy stated. This personalized approach to serving the customer was contagious and often compelled his team to follow suit.

Randy's ability to lead by example and empower his team to cater to their customers led his store to be in the top ten in the company in several categories, including sales, which he has held consistently for several years. Randy is a great example of what leading by example can do for creating culture and how training your team to go above and beyond for the customer can lead to positive results.

---

16 Ibid.

Ultimately, culture is created by people, and nobody can influence culture more than leaders. Leaders have the ability to determine what type of culture will exist in their organization. The leaders who strive to WOW their customers by going above and beyond for them often perform well. The leaders who take it a step farther and hire and train people to embrace an empowered, customer-centric culture can maintain above-average levels of performance. Sprinkle firm and frequent doses of supervision and accountability into the mix, and I will show you an organization worth aspiring to replicate. Before taking that step as a leader, you must first realize that the necessary steps might be difficult to quantify. Here's why.

TANGIBLE VS. INTANGIBLE

Most people believe that a strategy of focusing on more tangible aspects of business will produce the greatest results. Let's take a look at the definition of tangible. Tangible means "Clear and definite; real."[17] Things like products, business location, finances, and even email inboxes consume the majority of a business leader's time. Why? Because these are tangible things—clear and definite things, as our definition for "tangible" clearly states. Leaders spend a disproportionate amount of their time focusing on tangible items, rather than intangibles like leadership and culture. Although difficult to measure, the intangibles in business can produce extraordinary results, which can lead to a competitive advantage.

---

17 "Tangible: Definition of Tangible by Lexico," Lexico Dictionaries, Accessed May 19, 2020.

In describing the importance of culture, author and management consultant Peter Drucker stated, "Culture eats strategy for breakfast." [18] Most entrepreneurs and leaders spend significant time thinking about strategy. Yet strategy will not be as effective as it can be without an appropriate culture at the core of that strategy. Part of the reason strategy is thought about more often than culture is because culture is more elusive and intangible than strategy.

The definition of intangible is: "Difficult or impossible to define or understand; vague and abstract."[19] In business, leadership can be considered abstract. You most likely know what leadership is, but there could be varying levels of understanding when it comes to the topic and its implementation. You and I could both share our understanding of leadership, but it is still considered an abstract type of term. The same can be said about culture. Culture is somewhat of an abstract concept—especially when you think of organizational culture. I believe this is why leaders do not focus on leadership and culture as much as they should.

Enron is a good example of an organization whose unethical leadership and poor culture led to its demise. Before their historic collapse, Enron was one of the largest companies in America.[20] If size and money determined long-term success, Enron might still be a powerhouse today. Instead, they

---

18 Kobulnicky, Ben. "Does Culture Really Eat Strategy?" Medium. Startup Grind, February 15, 2019.

19 "Intangible: Definition of Intangible by Lexico," Lexico Dictionaries, Accessed May 19, 2020.

20 Troy Segal, "Corporate Bankruptcy: An Overview," Investopedia, May 15, 2020.

are known as a primary case study in what not to do as a leader. The shady business practices by their senior leadership destroyed their business and personal reputations as they faced legal charges for fraud. Enron's collapse at the time was the biggest corporate bankruptcy in the world of finance.[21]

Although culture might eat strategy for breakfast, the two combined with solid leadership is a formidable opponent. Before we dive farther into how to create and leverage culture, let's define it first.

CULTURE DEFINED

To truly understand culture, let's begin by defining what it means. Culture is shared amongst people. Culture naturally helps prioritize tasks and responsibilities. Culture dictates where people place value. My definition of culture is: "The unwritten, yet commonly shared set of beliefs that guide behavior." If something is not written, then it is more difficult for it to be considered tangible.

Culture can be considered unspoken behaviors. Strategy, on the other hand, is a road map for arriving at a certain destination in the future. A good strategy is often one that includes tangible action steps that can be taken to accomplish a goal. This is a big reason why tangibles are focused on much more in business than intangibles like culture—you can see it, feel it, and touch it.

---

21 Troy Segal, "Enron Scandal: The Fall of a Wall Street Darling," Investopedia, May 4, 2020.

Culture can be a good thing or a bad thing. Thinking back to the differences in culture between the DC division and CI division, the responsibility sits directly with leadership. My CI vice president promoted a culture of empowerment, autonomy, and empathy. My DC vice president promoted a culture of work/life balance not being important and top-down leadership, which stifled communication, collaboration, and buy-in.

So, the question you have to ask yourself as a leader is not whether your organization has a culture or not but rather what type of culture does your organization have?

If you take it one step further, you should also ask what type of behavior your current culture promotes? If you can answer those questions, you can determine how you can positively impact behavior, which will lead to results.

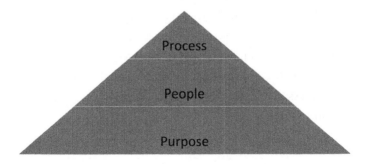

When it comes to organizational culture, there are three main components: purpose, people, and process:

1. **Purpose:** (Task Vs. Mission-Driven) Task-driven environments are very checklist heavy, compliance-oriented, and top-down leadership centric. Purpose-driven environments are where team members are inspired by a common mission, vision, and values.

2. **People:** (Collaborative vs. Competitive) Collaborative environments are highly integrated team efforts. Competitive environments are highly independent.

3. **Process:** (Status Quo vs. Innovate) Status quo environments live by the motto, "If it ain't broke, don't fix it." These environments are highly predictable and stable. Innovative environments, on the other hand, are highly flexible and encourage failing fast. Innovative cultures understand the importance of quickly adapting to change.

Culture can take on several different forms and impact people in a variety of ways. Here's a personal example of what I've seen culture do in my life and the lives of others.

CENTRAL INDIANA VS. WASHINGTON DC CONT.

My former vice president in CI understood the importance of connecting with people and motivating her team instead of leading them out of fear. She also made it a point to do the right thing—regardless of what a policy might state. A perfect example of this was how she handled a situation I brought to her attention shortly after accepting a job offer from them in the summer of 2012.

I had just found out that my grandfather passed away. He lived in Nigeria and the funeral services would be held in his hometown in Oyo State, Nigeria. With Nigeria being so far from the United States, my parents were planning to spend at least two to three weeks there. The problem was although I accepted the district manager position, I had not officially started the role. The vacation policy at the time stated that vacation time could not be used until after six months with the company, and even then, I would only have one week of vacation to use.

Although I knew it was very unlikely that I would be granted the vacation time in advance, I still decided to ask if she could do anything to help me witness the memorial of my grandfather. To my delight, she said yes! Not only did she approve the vacation time prior to me accruing it, but she also did not take that vacation time away from me. I was still entitled to my normal vacation time on top of the additional vacation time she granted. I could not believe it. That day I decided that I would do everything in my power to never let her down.

My CI vice president was a servant leader who got her people to elevate their performance because they did not want to disappoint her. This is the type of leadership that leads to an award-winning culture in which leaders understand that their job is to serve their teams, not the other way around. When leaders utilize a servant leadership style, they are showing their team they are valued. By serving your employees, you are making a deposit into your employees' emotional bank account. Over time, those emotional deposits will lead to a culture of loyalty, engagement, and above-average performance.

If you are or have been part of an organization similar to the CI division, you know what it is like to work in an outstanding culture. However, for the vast majority of us, we either have never been or currently are not part of a special culture. Over 80 percent of executives believe their company currently has the wrong culture.[22] So, if you find yourself in a position similar to the DC division and have a less than desirable culture, let's dive into practical ways to turn things around.

CULTURE AND PERFORMANCE

In the book *Start with Why* by Simon Sinek, he states:

"Great organizations become great because the people inside the organization feel protected. The strong sense of culture creates a sense of belonging and acts like a net. People come to work knowing that their bosses, colleagues, and the organization as a whole will look out for them. This results in reciprocal behavior. Individual decisions, efforts, and behaviors that support, benefit, and protect the long-term interest of the organization as a whole."[23]

Trust, vulnerability, accountability—these are all present in organizations with strong cultures. These characteristics create what I would consider healthy organizations.

In an article called "Note on Organizational Culture" by the Stanford Graduate School of Business, the authors describe

---

22 Graham Little, "Deloitte Human Capital Trends in Perspective."

23 Simon Sinek, *Start with Why: How Great Leaders Inspire Everyone to Take Action* (New York: Portfolio Penguin, 2019), Page 105.

the relationship between strong cultures and performance. The article goes on to highlight the significant amount of empirical research "that suggests that organizational cultures play a crucial role in shaping the capabilities of organizations and guiding the behavior of individuals within organizations."[24]

The authors of the article were able to discover that strong corporate cultures not only conclusively lead to higher firm performance but also those firms experience more consistency. The strong performance coupled with less volatility helps these firms sustain a competitive advantage in the marketplace. They defined a strong organizational culture as one where "basic assumptions of the culture are widely shared and deeply held by members of the organizations."[25]

Below are the three reasons why strong-culture firms outperform weak-culture firms:

1. **Social Control:** When firms are able to get strong cultures in place, the norms of the culture help positively influence behavior. In fact, research shows that "Corrective actions are more likely to come from other employees, regardless of their place in the formal hierarchy. Informal social control is therefore likely more effective and lower cost than formal control structures."[26]

---

24 Jesper Sorensen, "Note on Organizational Culture," Stanford Graduate School of Business, 2009.

25 Ibid.

26 Charles A. O'Reilly and Jennifer A. Chatman, "Culture as social control: corporations, culture and commitment," Research in Organizational Behavior 18: 157-200. 1996.

2. **Decision-Making:** When firms have strong corporate cultures in place, there tends to be better clarity around goals and decision-making. These characteristics are especially helpful when ambiguity is present in the workplace because efficiency is still captured by employees being able to make sound decisions in the face of uncertainty. In a body of work titled "Corporate culture and economic theory," author David M. Kreps, shared that "Goal alignment also facilitates coordination, as there is less room for debate between different parties about the firm's best interests."[27]

3. **Employee Engagement:** Firms with strong cultures tend to have employees who are actively engaged and motivated to perform. This sense of motivation and direction helps inspire employees, which creates a better atmosphere for accomplishing goals. The autonomy that often comes with strong corporate cultures allows for higher levels of engagement. In an article titled "Corporations, culture and commitment: Motivation and social control in organizations," author Charles A. O'Reilly stated that "Strong cultures can enhance employee motivation and performance due to the perception that behavior is more freely chosen."[28]

---

27 David M. Kreps, "Corporate culture and economic theory," Pg. 90-143 in J.E. Alt and K.A. Shepsle (eds.), Perspectives on Positive Political Economy Cambridge, England: Cambridge University Press, 1990.

28 Charles A. O'Reilly, "Corporations, culture and commitment: Motivation and social control in organizations," California Management Review 31: 9-25. 1989.

POTENTIAL PITFALLS

Hopefully, by now you all realize the value of having a strong organizational culture. The best leaders understand the role they play in creating and cultivating culture. Before we talk about the mission, vision, and values of your organization, let's quickly review a common pitfall of strong organizational cultures.

Authors Jesper B. Sorensen and Lynne G. Zucker shared in an article titled "The strength of corporate culture and the reliability of firm performance," that "...in general, strong corporate cultures encourage exploitation, at the expense of exploratory learning. One consequence of this is that the value of a strong corporate culture is contingent on the degree of change and volatility in a firm's competitive environment... while strong corporate cultures encourage performance reliability in stable environments, strong cultures may be a liability in volatile, rapidly changing environments. In this sense, strong organizational cultures may be a liability, particularly when the basic assumptions encoded in the culture conflict with evolving strategic realities."[29]

Knowing this is a common pitfall of a strong organizational culture, it's vital to create safeguards around those pitfalls. I believe change management is key to mitigating this risk. Structurally, I encourage companies to lean toward decentralized organizational structures when possible. When an organization is decentralized, it can make decisions much quicker than top-down organizations. The ability to make

---

29 Jesper B. Sorensen and Lynne G. Zucker, "The strength of corporate culture and the reliability of firm performance," Administrative Science Quarterly, 47: 70-91. 1977. 2002.

decisions quickly allows organizations to be more agile, which can lead to a competitive advantage. Implementing a flat organizational structure and decentralized process can allow you to overcome potential barriers that strong cultures can create.

Now that we have laid the foundation for what culture is, defined it from an organizational perspective, and described why it leads to strong performance, the next chapter will take a look at a story that showcases how a famous retail executive was able to turn the culture around for an iconic fashion brand.

***

CONTEXT

Culture is the unwritten, yet commonly shared set of beliefs that guide behavior. The responsibility of senior leadership is to influence and promote a healthy organizational culture, which can lead to superior performance compared to firms with weaker cultures. As a leader, you should strive to foster a customer-centric, empowered culture where team members are encouraged to say yes to customers whenever possible.

ACTIVITY:

1. What does culture mean to you? Take a moment to write down your personal definition of culture.
2. Describe the culture of your organization. If you are not a part of an organization, reflect on the culture of an

organization you aspire to be a part of. How does culture influence that organization?

3. Think about the culture you would want in your organization if you were the CEO. Take time to jot down some characteristics you would want people to associate with your company.

Picture This: A strong organizational culture with highly motivated and engaged employees is the result of leveraging the Circle of Leadership framework.

CHAPTER 2:

LEVERAGING CULTURE (80/20 RULE)

———

"Although transforming culture may feel somewhat elusive or even challenging, it is never too late to change culture."

—ANDREW ADENIYI

***

DARE TO LEAD

Stefan Larsson, former chief executive officer for Ralph Lauren Corporation, knew the value of leveraging culture to win. However, he never would have guessed that doing so would lead to an additional $1 billion in sales within three years at a struggling retailer.

In *Dare to Lead* by best-selling author Brené Brown, she shares a story about Stefan Larsson and how he "is credited with turning around the iconic American apparel brand Old

Navy, where he and his team delivered twelve straight quarters of growth."[30] Larsson was able to change the culture of the struggling retailer, which allowed the company to turn its performance around.

When Larsson was explaining how he was able to turn the company around, he talked about first starting with getting the team to refocus on its original purpose. By spending time learning what the initial vision for the organization was, Larsson was able to determine what direction he needed the organization to go. The next step in his transformation process revolved around improving the organization's health. According to Larsson, "The most crucial component to unlock and the biggest driver of success turned out to be transforming the organizational culture. What was once an entrepreneurial, fast-moving, and empowering culture had over the course of several years of struggling performance become hierarchal, siloed, political, and filled with fear."[31]

When you think about a large company failing, you may think of poor products, bad business model, or other tangible components. But Larsson and his team discovered that it all boiled down to the intangibles. Larsson goes on to state, "To turn the brand around, our main job was to build a culture of trust."[32] Larsson and his team were able to establish trust and increase communication throughout the organization by being intentional with fostering that culture.

---

30 Brené Brown, *Dare to Lead: Brave Work, Tough Conversations, Whole Hearts*, Random House Large Print Publishing, 2019.
31 Ibid.
32 Ibid.

By creating better systems for communicating, eliminating blame and judging, and encouraging continuous learning, Larsson was able to "enable openness, trust, and teamwork." [33] Larsson was able to eliminate the previous culture of avoiding failure and transformed it into one where risk-taking was encouraged. Ultimately, Larsson's leadership led to Old Navy outperforming competitors in their industry.

As you can see from Larsson's experience, the key was changing the company culture. He was able to accomplish this by allocating time toward discovering the purpose (vision) of the company, asking the right questions, and valuing the input of his team. These crucial steps enhanced communication, collaboration, and growth, which is precisely what the organization needed at the time. Although it was hard work for Larsson to turn things around, it was truly a small percentage of his time allocated toward the intangibles of business that really moved the needle.

Let's take a look at a simple concept that can help us all better tackle culture-related challenges within our own organizations.

80/20 RULE

The Pareto Principle states that the majority of things in life are not evenly distributed. The principle, which is also known as the 80/20 rule, states that 20 percent of your effort can lead to 80 percent of your results. The opposite is also considered to be true; 80 percent of your effort typically leads to only

---

33 Ibid.

20 percent of your results. "The Pareto Principle helps you realize that the majority of results come from a minority of inputs."[34]

I believe the Pareto Principle can be applied to the concept of culture and leadership. If you use the 80/20 principle and apply it toward creating and reinforcing culture, you will reap the benefits in the long run. As a leader, you should aim to dedicate at least 20 percent of your time to strengthening your organization's culture. If you can commit to that ratio, you'll eventually receive a return on your investment that will be well worth it.

Let's take a step back to consider the leadership at both divisions within the international grocery chain I used to work at. My CI vice president took the time to get to know you. Whether you were a part-time cashier or director of operations, she took pride in remembering things about you. She would often bring up the names of my employees' spouses or their kids when we would visit my stores. This display was impressive because she typically visited each of my stores once or twice a year and oversaw roughly 1,000 people.

Most leaders—especially those in her position—would forget the names of some of my managers' kids, yet she would remember to ask about significant upcoming life events, like a graduation. Did she have a far better memory than most? No, not necessarily. She simply put in more time and effort to make a personal connection with people. Her 20

34 "Understanding the Pareto Principle (The 80/20 Rule)," Better Explained, Accessed June 3, 2020.

percent consisted of her jotting down notes after each visit and reviewing those notes prior to entering a store she was about to visit. So even if six months passed between her visits, she could still pull up her notes before she walked into a store. Her intentionality around the intangibles like relationships and culture was her differentiator.

We are all capable of setting aside 20 percent of our time to invest in others to show our teams that we care. If you invest in your people, they will invest in you. My DC vice president did not have this relationship with his people. Not only would he forget names, but he would also forget things such as where you were at in your training, or even how long you had been with the company! It did not matter if you were a cashier or district manager. He was bound to not do anything to show he took effort in getting to know you as a person.

His failure to dedicate 20 percent of his time toward his people was a major reason why he did not have buy-in from people who reported to him. He led out of fear instead of respect. Nobody was willing to go the extra mile for him unless their job was on the line. And as a result, retention, employee engagement, and other performance indicators were substandard.

Is it truly 20 percent of your time that you need to set aside? Not precisely, but the bigger takeaway is that when a rather small percentage of your mental capacity is proactively focused on the long term, you give yourself and your organization a better chance of winning. Focusing on people and the intangibles of business will help you build the type of culture that will bring your organization long-term success.

If you're unsure exactly what that looks like, this next section will help.

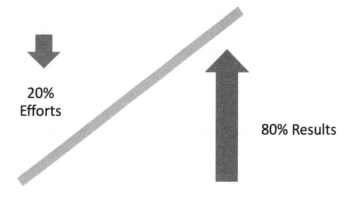

20% Efforts

80% Results

20 PERCENT TIME

The Pareto Principle is something some organizations have done a great job of incorporating into their culture. Google specifically has truly embraced what it means to place value in the 20 percent of things that should be a focus but often are not. As a company driven "to organize the world's information and make it universally accessible and useful."[35] Google has created a culture of innovation and creativity.

In the best-selling book titled *Drive* by Daniel Pink, Pink discusses how Google encourages its engineers to spend 20 percent of their week working on a project not associated with their primary job responsibilities. According to Pink, "Some Googlers use their '20 percent time' to fix an existing product, but most use it to develop something entirely new."

---

35 "About Google, Our Culture & Company News," Google, Accessed June 3, 2020.

Pink goes on to explain that "In a typical year, more than half of Google's new offerings are birthed during this period of pure autonomy."[36]

To think that an organization as accomplished as Google has had such a high percentage of their new offerings come from this 20 percent time is remarkable.

Below are some of the most notable creations birthed during Google's infamous 20 percent time:

- Google News
- Gmail
- Okurt (social networking software)
- Google Talk (instant message software)
- Google Sky (pictures of universe)
- Google Translate (mobile device translation software)

In *Drive*, Pink highlights statements made by an engineer from Google named Alec Proudfoot. Alec himself was able to work on a project centered around improving the efficiency of hybrid cars. Alec stated, "Just about all the good ideas here at Google have bubbled up from 20-percent time."[37]

If 20 percent of a typical Google employee's time can produce such great results, what could 20 percent of your time produce when directed toward the intangibles of business? Truly embracing this approach requires a leader who wants their team to innovate and have autonomy. If this is not feasible for

---

36 Daniel H. Pink, *Drive: The Surprising Truth about What Motivates Us*, Edinburgh: Canongate, 2011.

37 Ibid.

your organization or the culture of your organization, think about why that is. If a culture does not provide autonomy and innovation, is it adding value to your company or hindering it? Sounds good in theory, right? Let's talk through how to make this work in a more practical way.

80/20 PRINCIPLE APPLIED

While 20 percent of your workweek is my recommendation, it's not about a specific percentage of time but rather about proactively allocating time to do your best most strategic work—which should revolve around people.

So how can you apply "20-percent time" in your organization? Although the concept may seem straightforward, it does require intentionality, dedication, and strategy to execute. The approach is an investment. That can be difficult to quantify, which is a big reason why this concept is not even more widely practiced. This approach can be culturally challenging to adopt as well.

In *Drive*, Daniel Pink recommends calling the approach "20-percent time with training wheels."[38] If you begin the initiative in smaller more bite-sized pieces, it will be easier for your team to digest. For example, perhaps you can

---

38 Ibid.

rollout 5-10 percent time instead of 20-percent time. Another idea is to test the method within a particular department or team. This will help get buy-in that will eventually spread throughout your organization. You may realize there are some tweaks that you need to make to the plan for it to be effective, which is okay. A predetermined timeframe for executing the 20-percent time is another suggestion. Perhaps testing out the approach for a quarter or half the year could be an effective strategy.

One example of a slightly condensed version of the 20 percent time shared in *Drive* by Daniel Pink comes from software producer Intuit. According to Intuit's Vice President for Innovation, Roy Rosin, Intuit's 10-percent initiative "changed the culture in meaningful ways and created some very compelling results... After our CEO declared 'mobile' was key to our strategy, none of our business units were able to change direction on a dime, but our employees using 10-percent time created seven mobile apps before any formally funded mobile projects even got started." [39] The solutions created during the 10-percent time added much more value than the time investment dedicated toward those solutions. If something as popular and impactful as the post-it note can come from 20-percent time, what can you and your organization produce if given the same allotment of time for strategic work?

Twitter is another example. "In 2010, the company held a 'Hack Week'—an entire week when its employees 'built things that are separate from our normal work and not part

---

39   Ibid.

of our day-to-day jobs,'" according to Pink. [40] These small yet powerful time periods of increased autonomy allowed employees to have the bandwidth and flexibility to execute their good ideas. To lay the foundation for concepts like this to work, try to incorporate the following components:

1. Allow employees to work on whatever they want
2. Encourage collaboration and relationship building
3. Provide any resources and assistance needed

Pink also recommends you "impose just one rule: People must deliver something—a new idea, a prototype of a product, a better internal process—the following day." [41] By providing these ground rules and truly encouraging innovation, you may be pleasantly surprised with what you and your team can create. In closing, Pink shares that these days may "be the most powerful innovation practice in business today." [42]

Still unsure about how to best take advantage of 20-percent time? Let's look at leveraging culture from another perspective.

---

40   Ibid.
41   Ibid.
42   Ibid.

CULTURE > STRATEGY

If you are looking to change the current culture of your organization, I recommend you follow these five principles found in "Cultural Change That Sticks" by Jon R. Katzenbach, Ilona Steffen, and Caroline Kronley:[43]

1. Align organizational strategy and culture
2. Focus on key shifts in behavior
3. Reinforce current strengths of culture
4. Intertwine formal and informal initiatives
5. Measure and monitor progress

Changing organizational culture is difficult. It requires authenticity, hard work, strategy, and energy directed toward purpose, people, and process. One question to ask yourself as you are working to evolve your organization's culture is what behaviors would you like to see within the culture you aspire to foster? Let the answer to that question propel you and your team forward.

If you are starting a business, what practical steps can you take to create a culture from scratch? According to "The Leader's Guide to Corporate Culture: How to Manage the Eight Critical Elements of Organizational Life" by Boris Groysberg, Jeremiah Lee, Jesse Price, And J. Yo-Jud Cheng, there are four crucial steps:[44]

43   Jon R. Katzenbach, Ilona Steffen, and Caroline Kronley, "Cultural Change That Sticks," Harvard Business Review, November 27, 2019.
44   "Faculty & Research," Harvard Business School, Accessed June 3, 2020.

1. Articulate the aspiration
2. Select and develop leaders who align with the target culture
3. Use conversations to stimulate a sense of urgency around culture
4. Reinforce the desired culture through organizational design

This framework allows you as a leader to cast vision, develop a team around that vision, and reinforce that vision day-to-day. As an entrepreneur, you get the luxury of creating culture from scratch. What often happens in situations like that is the organization takes on a set of behaviors and characteristics similar to the founders'. This could be a good thing if the founders think about their future organization while making current business decisions. It could be a bad thing if the founders are terrible leaders and do not lead by example.

One of the key differences between creating culture from scratch and changing an existing culture is you do not have a framework to start with or alter. This could be a good thing or bad thing depending on how close the existing culture is to the desired culture you want to foster. In both situations, you must articulate the vision to your team and get buy-in from key leaders within the organization.

As the leader, it is also important for you to not only model the behavior you wish to see but frequently repeat the vision and the steps it will take to get there. People want to know where they are going and why that is the destination.

Circling back to the example of good and bad culture from one of my former organizations, my vice president from CI was able to obtain above-average results and knew the importance of reinforcing her vision. She also knew the importance of hiring leaders who also believed in her vision. Her emotional intelligence allowed her to get everyone in alignment to drive performance. My poor-performing vice president in DC never clearly articulated a compelling vision and did not have the right leadership team around him. The result was disjointed agendas and poorly communicated "whys" behind the "whats."

As we transition from leveraging culture to mobilizing your team around a singular purpose, let's review some key tips for creating an effective culture.

TIPS FOR CREATING AN EFFECTIVE CULTURE

Although transforming culture may feel somewhat elusive or even challenging, it is never too late to change culture.

However, you must understand that changing culture takes time and you must be intentional about the transformation. Below are tips for leaders on how to create and leverage an effective culture:

1. Keep your company structure as flat as possible to promote opportunities for collaboration, growth, and flexibility
2. Have a disciplined decision-making process that includes looking for disconfirming information. This type of information can be just as valuable, if not more valuable, than confirming information
3. Create a culture of open debate. Encourage playing Devil's Advocate
4. Create a culture where asking questions not answering them is valued
5. Institute a "pause and learn" mentality to decision-making and various projects
6. Leaders should publicly reward staff
7. Create a culture where people's ideas and concerns are truly considered prior to making a decision
8. Create a strategic planning process that is centered around issues
9. Encourage a listen to learn culture, not listen to respond
10. Create a culture of failing fast. Encourage resiliency

Improving the culture at your organization does not have to be an overwhelming experience. You simply need to be intentional. This can be accomplished by blocking out time on your calendar each week to connect with your team and grow your leadership skills. Now that the foundation for a healthy organization has been laid, it is time to start building. The building of a long-lasting, high-performing organization will depend on what I call the Three P's—Purpose, People, and Process. The next chapter kicks off the first of our Three P's—Purpose.

***

CONTEXT

Fostering the right organizational culture can lead to a sustainable advantage over your competitors. It is never too late to change culture, but you must be patient yet intentional to change culture. Take a proactive step toward changing your organization's culture by allocating a portion of your workweek to work on intangibles that will move the culture forward. Next, we will uncover the power of aligning your organization with a compelling and inspiring mission. When a rather small percentage of your mental capacity is proactively focused on the long term such as culture, you give yourself and your organization a better chance of winning.

ACTIVITY:

1. List three "20-percent activities" that you think could deliver an 80 percent return.
2. Do you believe strategy is more important than culture when it comes to business? Why or why not?
3. What are some steps you can take to positively influence the culture of your organization?

Picture This: Utilizing a systematic way to address culture will help ensure you are allocating adequate time toward purpose, people, and process.

PART 1:

PURPOSE

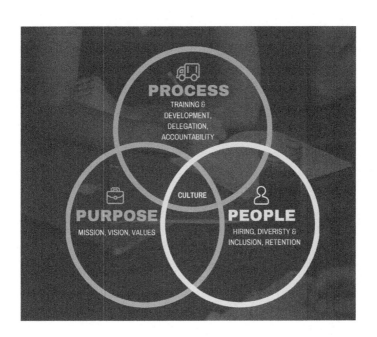

CHAPTER 3:

FINDING PURPOSE (MISSION STATEMENTS)

"When you know your why, you can endure any how."

−VIKTOR FRANKL

***

IGNITING FIRE

The question we should all be asking ourselves is "why"? Both individually and organizationally. The answer to that question should guide everything that you and your organization does. Although we all learn our "why" at different times and in different ways, each of our stories are important. The same holds true for John O' Leary; a man whose story I'll never forget.

Most nine-year-olds enjoy the simple things in life. Anything from playing sports, to video games, to interacting with friends is common with your typical pre-teen boy. However, what motivational speaker John O'Leary experienced as a nine-year-old boy was radically different. A combination of stupidity and a wild imagination led John to experiment with gasoline in his parents' garage. In the blink of an eye, John's home was not only engulfed in flames, but his body was covered in fire as well. The fire John started during his childhood caused significant damage to his body. According to John, 100 percent of his body was burned, and the prognosis for his survival did not look good.

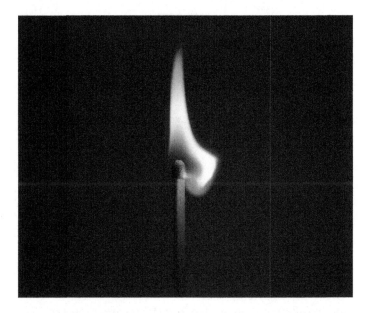

John shared his story on episode #119 of *The Entreleadership Podcast*. During his interview with host Ken Coleman, he shared the impact of people knowing their "why." John recalled his doctor (Dr. Raj) coming to his bedside regularly and asking him how he really felt. The sincerity in Dr.

Raj's voice resonated with John and showed him that he truly cared about him. Dr. Raj also made sure the entire hospital staff that came into contact with John was aware of how important their role was in John's survival. According to John, his doctor "would guide the entire team through this process so that everybody understood the role that they were playing to keep this little boy alive, other doctors, other nurses, everybody."[45]

One particular example of Dr. Raj's ability to get everyone focused on their "why" was the impact he had on a custodian named Lavelle. Lavelle was most likely paid minimum wage, or very close to it, and would be overlooked by most doctors. However, Lavelle's role was arguably the most important due to infection being such a common killer of burn victims. The janitors are responsible for the cleanliness of the rooms in hospitals, and John's doctor knew that it would be a team effort to keep John alive.

John remembered Dr. Raj bringing Lavelle to his bedside every morning and telling him he was keeping John alive. John's doctor was being genuine in displaying his appreciation for the work Lavelle was doing and made sure to acknowledge him in front of John. The simple act of saying thank you and explaining why Lavelle's work mattered was a difference-maker in the quality of care John received. "What this doctor spoke to is what ultimately motivates all of us, and its purpose, its mission, its passion, [and] its cause [is] greater than itself," John stated.

---

45   Coleman, Ken. "#119: John O'Leary--Living an Inspired Life". Podcast. The Entreleadership Podcast, 2015.

John went on to reference his favorite quote, which comes from Viktor Frankl, a Holocaust survivor, "When you know your why, you can endure any how."[46] This powerful quote found in Viktor Frankl's book titled *Man's Search for Meaning* applies in more settings than just business. It's one thing to determine how you will consistently exercise or break a bad habit, but it's another thing to keep your "why" at the forefront of your mind.

Focusing on your "why" will allow you to reach your maximum potential and keep you engaged and inspired. "The mission needs to proceed the execution, always," according to John.

When describing his personal "why," John stated, "I will thrive because God demands it. My family deserves it, and the world is starved for it. So each day and every interaction all day long that is in front of me. It weighs in my heart, it pulls me forward, and it launches me into engaging in life again."[47] As an author and speaker, John uses his story to ignite a fire in others and help them discover their "why" each and every day.

Let's examine what "why" looks like through an organizational lens, beginning with a mission statement.

---

46 Ibid.
47 John O'Leary, "Inspirational Leadership," John O'Leary, April 6, 2020.

MISSION STATEMENTS

A mission statement is "A written declaration of an organization's core purpose and focus that normally remains unchanged over time. Properly crafted mission statements (1) serve as filters to separate what is important from what is not, (2) clearly state which markets will be served and how, and (3) communicate a sense of intended direction to the entire organization. A mission is different from a vision in that the former is the cause and the latter is the effect; a mission is something to be accomplished whereas a vision is something to be pursued for that accomplishment."[48] We will talk more about vision statements in the next chapter.

There are several takes on what a mission statement is and what it is not. The definition/explanation above is the most succinct and accurate description I have seen so far. Think of a mission statement as your purpose.

I want to emphasize that a mission statement not only tells you what you do and where you go, it also indirectly states what you do NOT do and where you do NOT go.

A mission statement helps you prioritize. Think of priorities as a filter to help you know when to say no. Your mission statement, also known as your purpose, tells you when to

---

48   "When Was the Last Time You Said This?" Business Dictionary, Accessed June 4, 2020.

say yes. You want to strive to achieve your mission and that goal should be fairly achievable. Effective mission statements tend to include three things:

1. What you do or what you will do
2. How you do it or how you will do it
3. Why you're doing it or how you plan to do it

Once your mission statement is solidified, it is important to ensure decisions made within the organization do not contradict your mission.

The alignment of decision-making and your mission in itself can serve as a competitive advantage.

A culture where decisions are made rapidly and are effective allows you to take advantage of opportunities to grow. Below is a personal mission statement that I crafted for myself years ago:

To inspire others by being as successful as possible so that I can use that as a means to show people how great God is.

This mission statement has helped guide my decisions and behavior. Let's break down why this statement has been so impactful in my life. If you recall from earlier, an effective mission statement describes what you do or will do, how you do it or will do it, and why you're doing it or plan to do it. Think "**What, How, and Why.**"

My *what* from my personal mission statement is "To inspire others." My *how* is "by being as successful as possible" and my *why* is "so that I can use that as a means to show people how great God is." I encourage you to practice creating a mission statement using these principles. Always remember your why when making decisions.

Let's take a look at the mission statement of an iconic brand—The Coca-Cola Company. Their mission statement is "To refresh the world in mind, body, and spirit. To inspire moments of optimism and happiness through our brands and actions."[49]

The **what** from Coca-Cola's mission statement is "To refresh the world in mind, body, and spirit."
The **how** is "through our brands and actions."
The **why** is "To inspire moments of optimism and happiness."

Now that we have covered mission statements from a personal and organizational lens, I'd like to share a brief personal story regarding my "why."

---

49 "18 Captivating Mission Statement Examples You Need to Read," Tampa Inbound Marketing Agency, Accessed May 20, 2020.

DWAYNE WADE

The passion that people have when they believe in a purpose is remarkable. Regardless of if we are talking sports, music, business, or anything between, knowing and aligning with the "why" behind things leads to much higher levels of engagement and more passionate behavior.

The opponent was the University of Kentucky. The setting was the Elite 8 of the NCAA Men's basketball tournament. Dwyane Wade had just pulled off a triple-double on the biggest stage of his life playing for Marquette University. At the time, only a handful of players had ever recorded a triple-double during the tournament known as March Madness. This is when I fell in love with Dwayne Wade's game.

Dwyane Wade went on to get drafted fifth overall in the 2003 NBA draft by the Miami Heat. Although Wade was an amazing player, he did not receive the recognition that fellow NBA stars Carmelo Anthony and LeBron James received. As a fan, this was bothersome to me. I felt like Wade was the underdog in his draft class even though he had earned the right to be considered the front runner.

As the starting shooting guard for my varsity basketball team in high school, I was a key member of the team. However, I was not the leading scorer, and therefore did not get as much appreciation as I thought I deserved. This was one of many things I could relate to when it came to Wade. Growing up, I modeled my game after Wade. Although I was not the best three-point shooter (similar to Wade), I was a very good defender and was able to drive past my opponents with ease. It did not take long for others to notice I played like Wade.

I can also remember hearing countless times how much I resembled Wade. I'm not sure I've ever truly seen the resemblance, but I've gotten that feedback from several people over the course of my life. I could go on and on about why Dwayne Wade was my favorite player, but that's not the point of bringing him up. The point is, I have a "why" when it comes to my reasoning for supporting him. From being an underdog and not getting the recognition he deserved, to similarities in our playing style, my "why" for supporting Wade is very strong. This clear understanding of why I support him leads to me being highly engaged in his success and motivated to support him as a fan.

Are you a fan of your organization? If not, perhaps your lack of passion and engagement is due to your leader, the workplace culture, or both?

CENTRAL INDIANA VS. WASHINGTON D.C. CONT.

What about the CI division allowed them to consistently achieve superior performance? CI did not have access to superior candidates. CI had no additional requirements to join, no higher barriers to entry than DC. However, the behavior and performance of both divisions were drastically different. How can a company with standard operating procedures have two divisions that are run so differently? If the expectations are clear throughout an organization, you would think there would not be that much variance.

In addition to the examples provided in previous chapters, my vice president of the CI division also had a clear mission for the division. Our goal was to set the standard for the entire company—to be looked at as the model and to pick up the slack—when other divisions did not perform well. We competed with ourselves. The vice president from the DC division did not have a mission. Or if he did, it was poorly communicated and was not executed. People want to know where they're going and why they're going there. A clear and consistent message or mission should serve that purpose.

GUIDE RAILS FOR ENGAGEMENT

As a change management expert with over thirty years of experience, Alex Muñoz has been helping clients solve problems from a variety of industries from manufacturing, to healthcare, to the non-profit sector. During my interview with Alex, he mentioned how he has specialized in leveraging technology to assist in turning organizations around, as well as assisting with start-ups.

When asked about his key takeaways from his time working with clients, he mentioned how problem-solving can be overwhelming from the clients' point of view. However, given the fact that all organizations have problems that need solved, he sees a significant need to add this value to organizations. Alex's approach is to dissect issues into bite-sized chunks and teach his clients how to solve problems. "Everybody needs to learn how to solve problems," Alex stated during our interview. However, he often sees a disconnect with leaders utilizing their purpose to solve their problems.

The organizations with strong missions and engaged leaders tend to deliver the best results. Alex stated, "If you can help somebody understand their purpose and be able to really wrap their arms around, it will help them tremendously." The power of leveraging your purpose serves as what Alex calls "guide rails for our engagement." Before we dive into vision statements, let's ensure we know how to turn a mission statement into reality.

TURNING MISSION INTO REALITY

Although crafting a well-thought-out mission statement is vital; organizations often fail to get them to stick. If you were to take a poll at your current organization and ask how many people have memorized the mission statement, you'd quickly realize how few people can recite it on command. This is very problematic when the goal is to align decision-making with your "why." If your team cannot remember the "why" and be unified in driving toward that purpose, you will not reach your potential as an organization.

In an article titled "Turning Mission Statements into Action," author Tom Brown outlines how leaders can turn mission statements into reality.[50] His checklist is listed below:

1. "Make a concrete statement about what we will do and why"
2. "Move through 5 phases: iteration, awareness, understanding, commitment, and action."
3. "Each stage requires more effort than the previous one."
4. "Imagine a future reality": how will work get done?
5. Senior leadership must "explain, clarify," and reinforce how the statement will get implemented operationally
6. "Majority of employees should agree and align with" mission statement
7. "The complete knitting together of the purpose, direction, and behavior"

One point that I would add to the list is to make the mission statement memorable. If your mission statement includes a bunch of business jargon or is too long, it will likely not stick in the minds of your team. The more organic and simpler your statement can be, the better.

If someone asks you what your organization does, your mission statement should be the most simplistic way to answer that question.

---

50   Tom Brown, "Turning Mission Statements into Action," Accessed June 4, 2020.

***

CONTEXT

In summary, a mission statement serves as your core purpose; the how, what, and why you do what you do. To turn your mission into reality, you must continuously articulate the mission to create awareness and understanding in an effort to gain commitment and action. If you are able to successfully move through the five phases of bringing a mission statement to life (iteration, awareness, understanding, commitment, and action), you will position your organization to create and sustain a competitive advantage in the marketplace.

ACTIVITY:

1. Take a few minutes to create a personal mission statement. What is your purpose? Why do you think you exist?
2. What are you most passionate about? How can you align your passions with your daily activity?
3. What is the end goal of continuously pursuing your mission?

Picture This: Every organization and individual should be in constant pursuit of their mission. To pursue that mission, you must be clear about what you do, how you do it, and most importantly, why you are doing it. This is the first critical step to the "Purpose" component of The Circle of Leadership framework.

CHAPTER 4:

VISION AND VALUES

———

"People don't buy WHAT you do, they buy WHY you do it."
—SIMON SINEK

***

Now that we have established what a mission statement is, let's continue exploring the foundation of an organization's "why" by looking at vision statements and core values.

DR. SANJAY GUPTA

Transformative leadership is more of an exception than the rule. Although leaders usually do not intend to be poor leaders, they often are due to their own background and personal experiences. Often leaders lack the self-awareness necessary to realize their shortcomings. Other times leaders do not have people around them who are willing to be honest with them and provide constructive criticism.

In order to lead thousands of students and faculty at one of the largest institutions in America, you might assume charisma and confidence are among the most important qualities a good leader must exemplify. While you certainly need to be competent and have effective communication skills, Dr. Sanjay Gupta believes there are things even more critical. As Dean of the Eli Broad College of Business at Michigan State University, Dr. Sanjay Gupta knows a thing or two about leadership. I was impressed with his willingness to step into such a large role and knew he would be a great person to interview regarding leadership and culture.

"Many people have charisma but that's not enough. An ethical mindset is another cornerstone of a leader to deliver on tremendous results or outcomes," according to Dr. Gupta. Leadership plays a pivotal role in the success of any organization. If you are not inspirational as a leader, you are probably lacking a vision that is compelling and motivating to your team. One way Dr. Gupta believes this can be accomplished is by "being able to paint a picture or a vision about the future that is exciting, challenging, and rewarding." Casting a vision is important for getting a team to follow you as a leader. People want to know where they are going, why they are going there, and how they will get there. The process of executing that vision is equally important, or else you will have a bunch of dreamers on your team with no action taking place.

Dr. Gupta explained how he once thought that "institutions and organizations are very resilient and can transcend individuals." However, over the course of his career, Dr. Gupta started to recognize "leaders play a huge role in shaping the culture of the organization." In order to effectively shape the culture, leaders must lead by example. It is not enough to simply talk about the culture you want to have. You also need to model that behavior. The old saying of "actions speak louder than words" applies to leadership and culture as well. Dr. Gupta notes it is "very difficult to establish any culture without living it out yourself."

While Dr. Gupta has been fortunate to experience good leadership, he described a situation he recalled as a poor leadership experience where "the desire for exceptionalism was being challenged by a rush for mediocrity." Out of discretion, Dr. Gupta did not share a tremendous amount of detail surrounding the poor leadership experience, but he did share that many times poor leadership is not due to bad intentions. Poor leadership is what he describes as the "opposite of inspirational leadership."

SHINE
One major pitfall that Dr. Gupta has seen in examples of poor leadership is where subordinates are not given ample credit for their contributions. When the leader takes the "shine" for a job well done instead of deflecting that attention toward their team, it can be demoralizing. It is very difficult to improve morale and have a healthy organizational culture when your team has to question if you have their best interest at heart.

I have seen this firsthand as early on in my career, I once had a store manager complain to me about one of my peers (another district manager). Their main frustration? Their leader always took the credit if the store looked good when the director of operations visited. Not only did this create animosity between my peer and their store manager, but it also made my peer come across as arrogant to their leader.

Nobody won as a result of my peer not redirecting the attention toward their hard-working store manager. I learned at that moment the importance of being humble and giving credit where credit is due. It will naturally benefit you since you are ultimately held responsible for the performance of your team.

To close out our interview, Dr. Gupta stated that one piece of encouragement he would give to leaders and entrepreneurs is "aim higher and do better." His short and impactful advice displayed the importance of casting a vision and creating a culture of continuous improvement and results. A vision that motivates, inspires, and elevates performance will allow leaders to drive their team toward a common purpose. Although mission statements and vision statements are often considered interchangeable, there are distinct differences between the two. Let's compare and contrast.

VISION STATEMENTS

While mission statements are very practical and applicable, vision statements are more aspirational and challenging.

Best-selling author Simon Sinek describes vision in his book *Start with Why* as "the public statement of the founder's intent, WHY the company exists. It is literally the vision of a future that does not yet exist." Sinek goes on to state that "Average companies give their people something to work on. In contrast, the most innovative organizations give their people something to work toward."[51]

---

51 Simon Sinek, *Start with Why: How Great Leaders Get Everyone on the Same Page*, New York: Portfolio, 2009.

Think of a mission statement more like an explanation for what your company does, and think of a vision statement as something that has yet to be accomplished. For reference, below are side-by-side comparisons of vision and mission statements from my consulting firm AAA Solutions and a non-profit called Feeding America.

AAA Solutions
Mission:
To help small businesses win by amplifying their purpose, developing their people, and simplifying their processes.
Vision:
To help all small businesses in the world succeed.

Feeding America
"Mission: Our mission is to feed America's hungry through a nationwide network of member food banks and engage our country in the fight to end hunger."
"Vision: A hunger-free America."[52]

As you can see from the examples, Feeding America's mission statement explains what the organization does ("feed America's hungry") and how they do it ("through a nationwide network of member food banks") while the vision provides a compelling, future-oriented goal ("A hunger-free America").

A vision statement should excite, engage, and empower.

---

52 "18 Captivating Mission Statement Examples You Need to Read," Tampa Inbound Marketing Agency, Accessed May 20, 2020.

Let's look at a famous example of one of the greatest movements in American history. This movement changed the course of history and it all started with a vision.

I HAVE A DREAM

Dr. Martin Luther King Jr. is widely known as a catalyst in the civil rights movement. Dr. King was able to unite people from various backgrounds to come together for a singular focus. He understood the power of "why." He was consistent and inspirational in his approach toward accomplishing his goal: equality for all humans.

The transformation that Dr. King was able to initiate started with an emotional appeal called "I Have a Dream." Dr. King's dream consisted of equality for all, regardless of race. Dr. King's dream resonated in the hearts of millions. Dr. King was successful at casting a vision and motivating people to march toward that vision. His legacy lives on today, as he has a day in January named after him. Dr. King also has several streets in America that bear his name, among other accomplishments.

Although Dr. King was an excellent leader and public speaker, you also can get people behind a singular focus. You can cast a vision that is emotionally appealing and future-focused. The key is to start with "why" and make sure your vision statement is memorable and applicable to the people you want to bring together. Too often organizations make vision statements that apply only to the wider world instead of their employees. Visions are designed for those who you hope to be inspired by the statement.

Although this knowledge is foundational for leaders to understand when it comes to vision statements, what I will cover next is what will truly equip you with the tools to foster an excellent culture in your organization.

CORE IDEOLOGY AND ENVISIONED FUTURE

Visions are extremely difficult to achieve and are future-focused. Your vision statement should stand the test of time and serve as a compass for your organization.

> If your vision statement does not inspire action from your team, it is not ambitious enough.

According to an article in *Harvard Business Review* titled "Building Your Company's Vision," "Visions that are built to last include core ideology and envisioned future. Core Ideology: core values help navigate company and core purpose is a company's reason for being. Envisioned Future: ambitious plans to motivate the organization (ten-thirty years) and vivid descriptions of what achievement looks like."[53]

Let's look at the vision statements for a couple of highly successful companies:

---

53   Jim Collins and Jerry I. Porras, "Building Your Company's Vision," Harvard Business Review, January 19, 2016.

"To become the world's most loved, most flown, and most profitable airline." – Southwest Airlines[54]

"To bring inspiration and innovation to every athlete in the world." – Nike[55]

If you look at the longevity and company performance for Nike and Southwest Airlines, it's easy to see the success they have been able to obtain. Southwest is considered an innovator and leader in the airline industry, and Nike has been the leading footwear and apparel company for years. There are many reasons why these companies have been successful but having a purpose-driven culture coupled with a challenging vision statement has certainly aided in their long-term success.

Now that we have seen some examples, let's see what Harvard Business School has to say about vision statements.

THE VISION THING

According to an article published in *The Harvard Business Review* titled "The Vision Thing," a "Vision statement incorporates four elements: (1) customer orientation, (2) employee focus, (3) organizational competencies, and (4) standards of excellence."[56] Let's run one of our example vision statements through this framework.

---

54 Leonard Evans, "Southwest Airlines Co.'s Mission Statement & Vision Statement (An Analysis)," Panmore Institute, May 30, 2019.

55 Msa. "Nike Mission Statement 2020: Nike Mission & Vision Analysis," Mission Statement Academy, May 12, 2020.

56 Todd D. Jick, "The Vision Thing," Harvard Business Review, September 26, 1989.

When you examine Nike's vision, its customer orientation pertains to "every athlete in the world." The company goes on to define an athlete as any human with a body. The employee focus and organizational competencies in Nike's vision is "to bring inspiration and innovation." [57] These are clearly the things that the organization values and wants its employees to pursue. Lastly, the magnitude of Nike's vision statement displays its standard for excellence. To them, success is inspiring every human with a body (athlete) in the world. If that is not a lofty goal, I do not know what is.

Although many organizations have vision statements, not all visions are created equal. For the vision statements that do everything but inspire people, let's review why.

VISION PITFALLS

Now that we have discussed what a good vision statement should include and look like, let's turn our attention toward what visions should not look like. Below are common pitfalls of vision statements:

- Difficult to understand/too complex
- Difficult to memorize/too long or wordy
- Easily attainable
- Too narrowly focused
- Not actionable

---

57 Msa. "Nike Mission Statement 2020: Nike Mission & Vision Analysis," Mission Statement Academy, May 12, 2020.

With these common pitfalls in mind, let's unpack how a poorly written vision statement would have looked like for Southwest Airlines. Imagine if Southwest had a vision statement that was seven sentences long instead of one. The statement would certainly be too long to memorize, and that in itself would most likely stifle action. If the vision for Southwest was to be loved, flown, and profitable instead of "the world's most loved, most flown, and most profitable airline," their vision would be easily attainable and therefore too narrowly focused.

Southwest understood the importance of a memorable vision statement. They understood that a vision statement should include core ideology as well as an envisioned future. They understood the value of being oriented toward customers while staying focused on employees, organizational competencies, and standards of excellence.

If your vision is the destination and your mission is your set of directions, your core values are your means of transportation.

Now that we have walked through mission statements and vision statements, let's put the final piece to the puzzle when it comes to purpose.

CORE VALUES

The final component when it comes to focusing on your "why" is to solidify a set of core values. Core values help you turn passion into purpose. They help your team prioritize and help with engagement. Core values also help clarify your purpose, which can turn the mundane into the meaningful.

Research has shown that the most successful companies tend to have three to five core values. Anything more than five values can make it difficult for employees to memorize. As we learned earlier with mission and vision statements, you want employees to be able to easily remember the "why" of the organization.

When it comes to fostering an award-winning culture, core values should play a major role in what culture you want to build. Core values serve all of the following purposes:

- Articulate to customers and potential candidates what the organization values
- List what employees will be evaluated against
- Serve as a reminder of company culture
- Help guide decision-making
- Make the "why" clear

Thinking about behavior is important when determining your organization's core values. I always encourage entrepreneurs to choose values that are naturally important to them. This will make it easier for your values to stick.

As a leader, you must not only talk about what's important, but you must also display it.

To make this process more organic, think about what you value as an individual and brainstorm which of those values would be beneficial in an organizational setting. If your core values positively influence behavior, those values will help your organization achieve results.

Below are my personal core values that I look for in an organization prior to joining:

- Efficiency
- Growth
- Autonomy
- Simplicity
- Consistency

These values are non-negotiables for me and help me in my decision-making process. Now that I have shown you mine, what are your personal core values? What are the values of your organization? A man who I consider to be on The Mount Rushmore of Leadership believes core values are critical, and you should too.

PRESERVE THE CORE, STIMULATE PROGRESS

While a professor for the Stanford Graduate School of Business in 1988, Jim Collins's curiosity for discovering what made great companies tick began. In an episode of *The Entreleadership Podcast* titled "#130: How to Build an Enduring, Great Company," Jim recalled inheriting a course centered around small business and entrepreneurship. During the early stages of the course, Collins remembered reading the opening line of the syllabus and crossing it out. After putting a line through the opening sentence, he went on to write down what he truly wanted the class to explore, which was "how to turn an entrepreneurial venture or small business into an enduring great company."[58]

Although Collins did not know at that moment what the answer to that statement was, he was committed to finding it. "And that really launched the research that took twenty-five years and now has more than 6000 years of combined corporate history and the research database through the different studies. But it all goes back to that one moment where I wrote that down. By reframing it as how to build an enduring, great company as opposed to just running a business,"[59] Collins proclaimed.

After teaming up with his mentor and fellow professor at Stanford, Dr. Jerry Porras, Collins began researching visionary companies that changed the world, such as Disney, Walmart, and IBM. As a professor of Organizational Behavior and Change, Dr. Porras shared a similar passion

---

58 Colemen, Ken. "#130: Jim Collins--How to Build an Enduring, Great Company". Podcast. The Entreleadership Podcast, 2016.

59 Ibid.

and curiosity for what made companies reach the level of iconic as Collins did and still does until this day.

The six-year research process led to a few major findings. What Collins refers to as "one of the most enduring ideas" that came from the research was the concept of "preserving the core and stimulating progress."[60]

Collins and Dr. Porras found that regardless of the organization or industry, in order to endure as great, both preservation of core and stimulating of progress needed to be present.

According to Collins, preserving the core "means you have to be really driven by a set of core values. They're not open for negotiation. They're not open for discussion. They're not open for change."[61] Collins also went on to explain during his podcast interview that the core should define who you are, not what you do. This is something business leaders need to focus more time on. When a leader can get their entire team truly understanding why they exist and why the work they do matters, good things will happen. Walt Disney is an example of someone using money and business to fuel their purpose rather than allowing money or financials to serve as the purpose.

---

60 Ibid.
61 Ibid.

In addition to preserving the core, Collins also explains the other side of the equation, which is to stimulate progress. Collins goes on to define this concept as "to be constantly stimulating change and improvement in innovation and renewal. Always evolving your practices and your strategies as the world around you changes."[62] The combination of staying true to who you are while constantly evolving is a balancing act, and when executed correctly can make good organizations into great ones. This laser focus on preserving your purpose while pushing boundaries creates a culture over time of disciplined direction. Collins goes on to state that "a great company is marked by a culture of discipline, self-disciplined people who engage in disciplined thought and take disciplined action."[63]

All companies have a culture. The question leaders need to ask themselves is what type of culture do they have, and what type of culture do they want to have? The research done by Collins and Dr. Porras have solidified that a culture of discipline, preserving the core, and stimulating progress is a winning formula. Prioritize purpose and people over profit and you will have a solid organizational culture to build your company on.

***

---

62 Ibid.
63 Ibid.

CONTEXT

Let's take a moment to debrief what we have learned so far. Culture is the unwritten, yet commonly shared set of beliefs that guide behavior. Organizations that are able to spend a portion of their time focusing on culture can better leverage culture to drive results. I believe that spending roughly 20 percent of your time on reinforcing positive behaviors can lead to 80 percent of the performance of a company.

In order to create an award-winning culture, you must have a solid foundation. A compelling and easy to remember mission, vision, and set of core values help articulate the "why" behind your organization. Clearly defining your "why" can engage your workforce and aid in the decision-making process. Take some time to reflect on the impact of an effective culture and an inspiring purpose. It is important to understand the value of culture before we discuss the right approach to bringing people on your team.

ACTIVITY:

1. Take a few minutes to create or review your organization's vision statement.
2. What are your core values? Jot down three to five words that serve as your guiding principles.
3. What's a big audacious goal that can serve as your vision statement?

Picture This: Articulating your WHY through a compelling mission, vision, and set of core values help influence behavior and decision-making. Vision and values complete the "Purpose" section of The Circle of Leadership framework.

PART 2:

PEOPLE

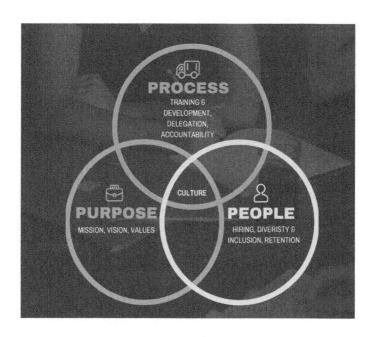

CHAPTER 5:

HIRING

"Leaders of great companies ask: first who, then what?"

–JIM COLLINS

***

LEE COCKERELL (THE DISNEY WAY)

Not only do companies often fail to hire the right person for the job, but they also fail to adequately train them. This is something The Walt Disney Company does not struggle with. The attention that Disney gives to their team members allows them to focus on the needs of the guests. The sense of pride in customer satisfaction is something that is embedded within the culture at Disney.

Theme parks, cartoons, movies, and toys are all symbolic items when you hear the name The Walt Disney Company. While these are all certainly components of Disney, there is much more that goes on behind the scenes to make Disney what it is today. I must admit that the simplicity behind Disney's key ingredients blew my mind.

On an episode of *The Entreleadership Podcast* titled "#115: Creating Leadership Magic the Disney Way," host Ken Coleman interviewed former Executive Vice President of Operations for Disney, Lee Cockerell. During his time at Disney, Cockerell oversaw 40,000 employees, which the company refers to as "Cast Members" and was in charge of twenty of the company's hotels, four of their theme parks, two of their water parks, a shopping and entertainment village, and the ESPN sports and recreation complex.

When asked about what made the culture at Disney so special, Cockerell stated, "When you come to Disney, number one, we hire better. We hire better people. We take our time, we hire people with the right attitude, a can-do attitude, not a can't-do attitude."[64] As my Circle of Leadership model indicates, one of the first steps to creating and leveraging culture is by hiring the right people. There are countless examples of successful companies attributing a large portion of their success to their people, and Disney is one of them.

The second step in my Circle of Leadership model centers around training. After referencing the prioritization that Disney has on hiring, Cockerell went on to say that another thing Disney does better than most when it comes to culture is training. According to Cockerell, "We train them, we test them, and then we enforce the training to make sure we have

64 Coleman, Ken. "#115: Creating Leadership Magic the Disney Way". Podcast. The Entreleadership Podcast, 2015.

consistency. There's total clarity when somebody is hired at Disney about expectations for performance and taking care of the customer."[65] The clarity that Disney provides to its cast members allows them to be laser-focused on customer service.

"Every customer matters," said Cockerell when talking about the millions of people Disney interacts with. However, the company trains its people to engage with guests individually.[66] Cockerell also believes, "Culture eats strategy for lunch. You get the culture right, your people will help you implement any strategy you come up with. If you don't get the culture right, you're not going to get anywhere because they're not going to help you, then they're going to quit. They're going to turn over. We want people to wake up in the morning, come into Disney knowing they matter, and we make sure they know they matter, no matter what position they have. From the lowest level to the highest level, you matter, you're a part of this."[67]

The key to great organizational culture is simple. However, many companies don't execute on the basics.

FOCUS ON BASICS

Cockerell states that any company can build a successful culture if they "don't get bored with the basics, you know, hiring, training, and creating a culture where people feel

---

65 Ibid.
66 Ibid.
67 Ibid.

appreciated."[68] Disney has been able to maintain a competitive advantage in the marketplace due to its culture, which is reinforced through its people. The philosophy that Cockerell explained can be summarized as "manage like a mother,"[69] according to Cockerell. Cockerell goes on to explain that mothers are typically worried about two things, safety and education. These are also two things that the leaders at Disney are expected to focus on as well. Education helps the team members grow and have a better life and safety allows them to continue coming to work and doing their best work.

Treating customers like individuals is another way that Disney focuses on people. "Treat people as individuals because companies who can individualize and personalize, I can tell you 100 percent are going to win in the long run," Cockerell said.[70] Respect and attention to detail are also important to Disney. "The attention to detail at Disney is just incredible," said Cockerell.[71] He went on to explain how everything mattered to the company and how that influences the service that guests experience.

To summarize, you must hire better and train better than your competitors in order to stand out. Set high expectations, clarify those expectations, and help your team grow to the best of your ability while paying excruciating attention to detail. This is the formula that worked for Disney, and it can also work for your organization. Let's get practical with how to focus on hiring. What if I told you the key to successful

---

68 Ibid.
69 Ibid.
70 Ibid.
71 Ibid.

hiring can be found in the contents of a bus? Continue reading and I will explain how.

GOOD TO GREAT

In a book titled *Good to Great* by best-selling author, Jim Collins, Collins explains that "Leaders of great companies ask: first who, then what?"[72] The premise of this approach is one centered in people coming before anything else. Regardless of how impactful your mission, vision, or core values are, if you do not have the right people to execute, you will not have long-term success.

---

72   James C. Collins, *Good to Great: Why Some Companies Make the Leap... and Others Don't*, New York, NY: Collins, 2009.

Jim Collins utilizes a bus metaphor to describe what an effective hiring process should entail from a leadership and business perspective. Collins describes a bus as a business and the bus driver is you as the leader. In order to get your company (the bus) to the right destination, he urges leaders to determine who will be on and off the bus prior to beginning your journey. He also recommends that leaders determine where team members will sit on the bus (in the company) prior to moving in a particular direction.

Below are the four major steps outlined in *Good to Great* by Jim Collins:

1. Get the right people on the bus

Selecting the right candidate is the first major step toward building a championship team. You can avoid a plethora of problems if you do this step correctly. It is crucial to slow down the hiring process so you can truly get to know applicants. By being consistent and thorough throughout the hiring process, you give yourself a great opportunity to discover red flags with candidates. You should make sure you do not fabricate the position to sell candidates on the opportunity. You want to be transparent about the challenges they will face in the position. Just as you are evaluating if the candidate is a good fit for the company, the candidate is evaluating fit between themselves and the organization. Transparency is key.

2. Get the right people in the right seats

Aligning skillsets, experiences, and personalities with the correct roles is very important. A candidate may be a good fit for the organization but a terrible fit for the position you are considering them for. Take time to get people who you are confident can perform the roles and responsibilities of the position you are hiring for. This is particularly important for senior leadership positions. You want your leadership team to believe in the vision of the company and be able to complement the strengths of the existing team. When a new hire is struggling in their role, you should consider if they are in the right position prior to taking steps to get them out of the company. Retention should be a focus for all organizations, and by evaluating if someone is in the right seat on the bus, you may find you have the right person, but they are in the wrong seat.

3. Get the wrong people off the bus
If an employee is struggling even after you have coached them, provided support for them to succeed, and considered a switch in position, it is time to consider getting them off the bus. The morale of your better performing team members will be in jeopardy if you do not pull the trigger on poor performers. The key is to be fair and consistent when handling performance issues. You want all people who exit your company to leave with a good perception of your company. Once you have terminated an employee, make sure to reflect on what went wrong so you can avoid making a hiring decision like that in the future.

4. Who before what
People decisions should take priority over all other decisions. If you focus on your team, they will focus on your customers, and the rest will take care of itself.

Be systematic with bringing people on the bus, intense with getting the wrong people off the bus, and openminded with getting them in the right seats.

Be forward-thinking and consistent from start to finish, and you will make good decisions when it comes to your biggest assets.

TAKE YOUR TIME

"Take your time with hiring!" was a statement I heard all throughout my training process at my first job after college, yet I had to learn that lesson the hard way. In my first year with hiring and firing responsibilities, I found myself running out of time to get one of my stores staffed for the fourth quarter—the last three months of the fiscal year. In a crunch for time, I found myself lowering my standards when hiring candidates. What used to be red flags were things I was willing to be lenient on. Before I knew it, I had hired half a dozen candidates that I probably would have passed on had I not been in a bind to bring people on board.

Although I had met my goal for staffing for that particular store, the aftermath of my poor hiring decisions was devastating. The end result was an increase in customer complaints, turnover from the new hires and some existing team members, and a decrease in overall store performance. After the quarter, I found myself in a worse staffing situation than before I hired the new people. This was when the statement,

"Take your time with hiring" finally hit me. Although I fully understand the magnitude of hiring, there are times when poor hiring decisions are made. And when you make a poor hire, you and the rest of your team are negatively impacted. Your customers will almost certainly be impacted by a poor hiring decision as well.

The fourth quarter is a very hectic time for most companies, especially those in retail. It can be a very fun and exciting time if you are adequately prepared and have the right people on the team. It can also be the most stressful time of the year if you are not appropriately staffed and do not have a good plan in place.

While terminating someone is one of my least favorite things to do as a leader, employing someone is one of the most fulfilling things. Giving someone the opportunity to earn money in order to provide for themselves and others is extremely rewarding. This is a responsibility I take very seriously, and you should too.

Dr. Phil Powell is a Clinical Associate Professor of Business Economics and Public Policy for the Kelley School of Business in Indianapolis, Indiana. Dr. Powell is also the Associate Dean of Academic Programs and a Daniel C. Smith Faculty Fellow. When interviewing Dr. Powell, he shared his philosophy on hiring, especially as it pertains to leadership and culture. "Hire people that you cannot keep up with," Dr. Powell stated. Dr. Powell believes that leaders often do not spend enough time on hiring, but when they do, they may not always hire tough enough. This is a common hiring pitfall that leaders must strive to avoid.

Change management expert Alex Muñoz also shared with me his thoughts on hiring and the impact it has on organizational culture. Alex said to "Fire fast, hire slow." The impact of a bad hire can be extremely detrimental to an organization, so Alex advises leaders to proactively set time aside to find talent. "It's better to limp than to make a bad hire in your organization," Alex stated.

The temporary discomfort you'll face as you take your time with hiring will be more advantageous in the long run than the discomfort and destruction that making a bad hire can cause.

One of the first steps to hiring effectively is recruiting and interviewing, however, most people are doing it wrong.

RECRUITING

One of the first steps in the hiring process is to determine what positions you need filled and what skills and abilities a candidate must possess in order to fill the position. Once you have identified your needs, you must recruit for the position by utilizing a job description to inform potential applicants of the responsibilities of the role.

There are several avenues you can take to recruit. I always recommend starting with employee referrals. Who better to explain the culture of the company and what it is like to work there than a current employee? You'll also find that good employees, for the most part, care about their reputation and would not recommend a candidate who they do not believe would do a good job. Offering bonuses and other incentives to employees who refer candidates to the job is another great way to encourage referrals.

Beyond employee referrals, I would recommend using a variety of online platforms to recruit for open positions. Platforms such as Indeed, Zip Recruiter, and even social media sites like LinkedIn can be very valuable. You can also explore in-person hiring events or career fairs. Preparation and adequate advertising for the event are both crucial for success. Tracking the results of your hiring options is a very smart way to determine which recruiting method yields the best results. You always want to know what kind of return on investment you get for your efforts. You'll eventually find what avenues work best for you through trial and error.

Hopefully, you understand the importance of recruiting as it gets the ball rolling in the hiring process. However, recruiting will never be as good as it can be if you are not prepared to interview candidates effectively. Let's take a look at the next phase of the hiring process.

INTERVIEWING

With over 2,000 interviews under my belt, I have learned a thing or two about hiring. Finding someone who can buy into what you believe in is not easy. The goal is to not settle for anything less than great candidates—not even good ones. Patience definitely needs to be practiced while progressing throughout the hiring process. It will take you time, but it will be time worth spending.

Below are my seven biggest interviewing tips based on experience:

1. Be patient
2. Be consistent
3. Be open-minded
4. Be intentional
5. Be transparent
6. Be informative
7. Be yourself

Patience in the interview process allows you to truly get to know a candidate. I recommend interviewing candidates at least two to three times. If you ask the right questions, after meeting with a candidate three times, you will have a good sense of who that person really is. You want to bypass the "interview show" that most people put on. Interacting with them multiple times will help reveal many things to you.

During an interview with the former Managing Director of Development for Teach for America, Mychael Spencer, he shared with me that "hiring is the most important job" for a leader. "People need to put more emphasis on hiring the right people," according to Spencer. As a former principal, Spencer saw first-hand the positive impact of making a good hire for someone on his team. "I don't want you to give me who you want to be, I want you to be who you are," stated Spencer. The moral of the story is if you are not rushing through the hiring process, you are much more likely to make a good decision.

Questions that evaluate the candidate's alignment with your organization's culture and purpose are vital. You also want the candidate to explain times where they have demonstrated qualities you may be looking for such as teamwork, creativity, and humility. Starting off questions by saying "Tell me about a time…" or "How would you handle…" allow you to get a better understanding of how the candidate has responded in the past or would respond should they encounter a particular situation in the future.

Consistency is also key when it comes to interviewing. It's hard to determine which candidate is best for a position if every candidate gets different questions. It's okay to ask follow-up questions to things that are brought up in the interview, however, you should strive to ask the same questions to each and every candidate. Consistency with what questions you ask not only makes hiring easier, it also helps you avoid getting into legal issues due to claims of discrimination.

Being transparent throughout the hiring process equips applicants with accurate information about the role and the company. Just like you are trying to determine if someone is a good fit for your organization, the applicant is also determining if the organization would be a good fit for them. Everyone wins when there is a mutual agreement regarding ability and fit. So, provide adequate information when it comes to what an applicant can expect if they were to get the role.

Try to create a disciplined interviewing culture. The first interview should be a culture-fit interview assuming your initial screening process is effective. If they don't fit the culture, you shouldn't want them on the team, regardless of skill set. Instead of simply asking questions, include some sort of activity or action in the interview process to get a further glimpse into how the candidate might perform in the role.

While determining if a candidate is competent is important, determining their emotional intelligence is even more critical for success.

EMOTIONAL INTELLIGENCE (EQ)

One recommendation I give hiring managers is to focus on emotional intelligence when hiring. Emotional intelligence is especially important when hiring leaders. In his article titled "What Makes A Leader?" Daniel Goleman talks about emotional intelligence and how that can distinguish great leaders from good leaders. Goleman defines EQ as "a group of five skills that enable the best leaders to maximize their own and their followers' performance."[73]

Goleman defines EQ skills as:

1. Self-awareness
2. Self-regulation
3. Motivation
4. Empathy
5. Social skill

If you can recruit and hire people with high levels of EQ, you can leverage your people to maximize their performance and

---

73   Daniel Goleman, "What Makes a Leader?" Harvard Business Review, July 18, 2017.

the performance of others. As you begin to recruit, interview, and eventually hire candidates, remember to select individuals who align with the "why" of your organization. Does this person share similar core values to my organization? Are they passionate about my vision? Are they inspired by the mission of the company? These are all questions you should get answered throughout the interview process. Best-selling author Simon Sinek said it best in his book *Start With Why*, "The goal is not to hire people who simply have a skill set you need, the goal is to hire people who believe what you believe."

Now it's time to practice.

HIRING TIPS

There are a plethora of strategies and tactics used to hire effectively. After reviewing research, reflecting on my personal experiences and experiences of others, I've created a five-step hiring process for professional positions. The steps are outlined below:

Step 1. Review Resumes

As a leader, you are most likely often in a crunch for time. By leveraging filtering tools, you can make the hiring process more efficient. By the time you start reviewing resumes, candidates should have already gone through some sort of screening process. Even if it's only a few questions asked when they submit their resume or application, anything to weed out candidates who will not be a good fit is recommended.

When you begin to scan resumes, look to ensure they meet the basic qualifications for the role you are interviewing for.

Also look for potential red flags like short stints with several employers or consistent sudden gaps in employment. You do not need to spend a significant amount of time reviewing someone's resume, but it is still an important step.

Step 2. 1st Round Phone/Virtual Interview
This step can take shape in a variety of ways. Anything from a phone call to a virtual video call can be a convenient tool when interviewing. Skype, FaceTime, Microsoft Teams, and platforms like Zoom can help accomplish a virtual interview, which will save your organization, as well as the applicant, time and money. My favorite virtual method is a platform called HireVue. HireVue is a pre-employment assessment and video interviewing tool that allows candidates to answer interview questions by recording them responding via video. This allows recruiters to review candidate responses without having to coordinate time to interview candidates live. There are significant efficiencies that can be captured by using virtual interviews and I have yet to see a more efficient tool than HireVue.

Step 3. DISC Assessment
The DISC assessment is a resource designed to improve productivity, teamwork, and communication. When used in the interview process, the DISC assessment can allow you to have a better understanding of who your candidates are and how they may mesh with other members of the team. When done right, a recruiter can use the results of the assessment to make better hiring decisions as the hiring process progresses.

Step 4. 2nd Round Phone/Virtual Interview

Step four consists of a virtual interview. This means that the first three steps of the hiring process do not have to require in-person human interaction. This is a huge time savings for any organization. Meanwhile, you can rest assured that only the best of the best have made it to the final rounds. During this virtual interview, DISC results should be discussed and alignment between the candidate and the company should be verified based on the candidate's personality, goals, experiences, cultural fit, and most importantly, ability to do the job.

Step 5. In-person interview with multiple people

The final round of the interview process should consist of the interviewee meeting with multiple interviewers. Regardless if you do a group interview or simple back to back rounds of individual interviews, you want a variety of people interacting with the applicant. I would recommend at least having a potential peer and an applicant's potential leader to interview during the interview process. Depending on your company structure, you may want your HR leader to interview applicants as well. Once this stage is completed, you should be in a position to offer jobs to the right people.

Approach hiring like you want to marry your applicants, not just date them. Hiring the right candidate is a pivotal step in minimizing turnover.

***

CONTEXT

Let's take a moment to debrief what we have learned so far. We began discussing the implications of a good and bad culture and then reviewed how a unified purpose can lead to results. Once your culture and a unified purpose are solidified, it's time to focus on building your team. Your people will be your greatest assets so you must be intentional and selective with who you hire.

In addition to being patient throughout the hiring process, it's crucial to be consistent and informative. The candidates you interview want to make sure your organization is a good fit for them and vice versa. Emotional intelligence has been proven to be a common denominator in effective leaders. Try to gauge potential leaders on their emotional intelligence ability during the interview process. Intentionality will help you select the right person for the right job. Remember to get rid of people on your team who are a cancer to the organization. Good performers will eventually leave your company if you do not get rid of the dead weight.

ACTIVITY:

1. If you were a CEO, where would you attempt to recruit your senior leadership team? What hiring methods do you think would yield the best results?
2. What kind of interview process would you implement in your organization? How many interviews? Who would conduct the interview? Would you interview them in person, over a video conference, or over a conference call?
3. What characteristics would you look for in a senior leadership team? How would you verify those characteristics?

Picture This: Think "who" before thinking "where." As a leader, it is your responsibility to make sure the right people are in the right seats on the bus. Be sure to get the wrong people off the bus or else the good ones will leave. Hiring is the first milestone within the "People" section of The Circle of Leadership framework.

CHAPTER 6:

DIVERSITY AND INCLUSION (D&I)

———

"If you think you are too small to make a difference, try sleeping with a mosquito."

—THE DALAI LAMA

***

PULL YOURSELF TOGETHER

As a self-identified lesbian and leader in corporate America, Kate Johnson has experienced the pressure of feeling the need to suppress who she truly was because of who she thought society wanted her to be. Kate worked for Duke University for seven years, served as a recruiter for McKinsey & Company, was the Director of Talent for boutique professional services firm FMI Corporation, and now works as a Senior Corporate Recruiter for Hyundai Motor Group.

Kate is also the author of *Pull Yourself Together*, a book about harnessing your differences and leveraging those differences to get ahead. Kate shares her story in *Pull Yourself Together*:

"At least that was a message I heard growing up. That my difference was too much. It wasn't just the decibels or the energy. It was the closeted queerness. It was my penchant for unbridled optimism in the midst of disaster. And for doing the things the opposite way of how other people were doing them. I am a lesbian born in North Carolina who had no idea how to launch or navigate her career with all that female-gay-bigness. I faced discrimination, prejudice, and tragedies at a young age. It was all compounded by my mother dying from cancer when I was nineteen."[74]

Unfortunately, many diverse people in America face difficulties at work with less-than-inclusive cultures and barriers in getting ahead. Kate gained momentum regarding how diversity and inclusion (D&I) should be fostered from her time at McKinsey. According to Kate, the global consulting firm has an organizational structure, confidentiality, and intensity similar to the military. "Every day they are working on some of the hardest problems on the planet," Kate stated during our conversation. The organization was making a conscious effort to exemplify D&I during her time there, which Kate appreciated. However, despite the D&I work being done at McKinsey, Kate believed there was even more that could and should be done.

---

74   Kate Johnson, *Pull Yourself Together: Owning Your Difference to Get Ahead*, New Degree Press, 2019.

Still very aware of her differences even in a thriving organization, Kate channeled her frustrations and creative spirit into writing her book. The book does an excellent job not only explaining what minorities go through in their careers but also offers solutions for how to harness differences to obtain a competitive advantage. Kate believes that basic leaders influence people, however, "great leaders influence and make people the best version of themselves." Below are "The Four E's" that Kate outlines in her book to give yourself a competitive advantage:[75]

- **Explore.** Find the personal and professional spaces you want to occupy."
- **Energize.** Generate the support, energy, inspiration, and drive to overcome opposition and prejudice."
- **Engage.** Opportunities always come. Prepare for them and leverage your toolkit when they arrive."
- **Expand.** Get in the game and test your limits!"

To summarize Kate's perspective, I would like to share a quote that she utilizes in her book:

"Your own Self-Realization is the greatest service you can render the world."—Ramana Maharshi[76]

Although Kate has taken excellent strides to help oppressed individuals take ownership of their differences, issues still exist with D&I in America. Despite the statistics that state businesses perform better when they have a diverse

---

75 Ibid.
76 Ibid.

workforce, there is still significant work that needs to be done. Let's discuss why that is, but first, let's define D&I.

DEFINING DIVERSITY AND INCLUSION (D&I)

So what exactly does D&I mean? I like to think of diversity as a numbers game from the standpoint of being able to measure or calculate it. While inclusion can be measured as well, it is much more about the impact on people. It is a feeling of trust and belonging. Technically speaking, "Diversity is the range of human differences, including but not limited to race, ethnicity, gender, gender identity, sexual orientation, age, social class, physical ability or attributes, religious or ethical values system, national origin, and political beliefs."[77]

Inclusion, on the other hand, "is involvement and empowerment, where the inherent worth and dignity of all people are recognized. An inclusive organization promotes and sustains a sense of belonging; it values and practices respect for the talents, beliefs, backgrounds, and ways of living of its members."[78]

As you can see from both definitions, D&I is centered around acknowledging and valuing differences between people. It's human nature to gravitate toward people who look, think, behave, and act like you. It's not as easy to connect with people who are different than you, therefore D&I takes work. The key is to recognize the value of putting forth the effort to improve D&I in your organization.

---

77 "Diversity and Inclusion Definitions," Ferris State University, Accessed May 20, 2020.

78 Ibid.

In an article written by Olivia Folick titled "Diversity & Inclusion: A Beginner's Guide for HR Professionals," she references research conducted by Deloitte that "finds that diversity is perceived differently by generations. Millennials view workplace diversity as the combining of different backgrounds, experiences, and perspectives, and they believe taking advantage of these differences is what leads to innovation. Gen Xers and Boomers, on the other hand, view workplace diversity as equal and fair representation regardless of demographics without necessarily considering diversity's relationship with business results."[79]

If you're looking to improve D&I, you must understand what it means to the people within your organization. Age, gender, and other factors can impact how people view D&I. A solid understanding of your people's perception of D&I will help you make decisions centered around the topic.

79 Mondal Somen, "Diversity and Inclusion: A Beginner's Guide for HR Professionals," Ideal, May 4, 2020.

D&I INITIATIVES TODAY

The makeup of the United States is changing rapidly. "Census Bureau projections show that the US population will be 'majority-minority' sometime between 2040 and 2050."[80]

> Therefore, the question you need to ask yourself is if the demographics of your company are representative of the customers you serve.

When I do D&I consulting for organizations, I always recommend striving for a workforce that mirrors the population you operate in. By doing this, you'll better serve clients, better recruit diverse candidates, and increase the chances of retaining employees for a long period of time, not to mention higher levels of organizational performance.

If the benefits of a diverse and inclusive workforce are so great and statistics clearly show a transition to a "white-minority" America, why do companies still struggle with D&I? Below are some reasons why D&I is not where it needs to be in America:

- There are not enough minorities in leadership positions in organizations
- A lack of support from senior leaders

---

80 "US Will Be 'Majority-Minority' in Next 25 Years," UPI, April 30, 2019.

- People not seeing the value in diverse and inclusive work environments

I once read that "minorities aren't heard until they make up at least 30 percent of the group." Although I am not sure about the accuracy of the statement, it appears to be true based on my experience, as well as the experiences of other minorities in my network. This is a dilemma that companies face all over the United States. The less diverse you are, the more difficult it is to recruit diverse candidates. This dilemma is all the more reason why diversity needs to be a focus of senior leadership—sooner rather than later—while the company is still small.

According to an article titled "Survey: What Diversity and Inclusion Policies Do Employees Actually Want?" by Matt Krentz, roughly 98 percent of large companies have diversity programs in place, yet 75 percent of employees surveyed felt no effect from the diversity programs.[81]

When implementing a D&I initiative, it is crucial not to implement the initiative simply to "check the box." If senior leadership is not behind the initiative, and there are no consequences for not embracing the change, the initiative will not work. Employees will see through the attempted rollout and it can have an even larger negative impact than not implementing a D&I strategy at all. Organizations that prioritize D&I often have the most engaging cultures. These cultures

---

81 Matt Krentz, "Survey: What Diversity and Inclusion Policies Do Employees Actually Want?" Harvard Business Review, February 5, 2019.

make you feel like your colleagues are family. This is exactly what I encountered at Starbucks.

STARBUCKS

As one of the most admired companies in the world, Starbucks is doing a lot of things right, and one of them is the way they approach diversity and inclusion. Every person matters and everyone deserves to be treated with dignity and respect.

As my leader wrapped up our two-day district manager meeting, I was speechless. Not only had I just witnessed a dynamic leader, but I had also experienced one of the most transparent and engaged teams I'd ever seen. And almost equally as impressive, in two days, we spent more time talking about diversity and inclusion than I spent in the seven years prior at other organizations. The icing on the cake was that I experienced all of this within my first week on the job. Starbucks not only talks the talk; they walk the walk.

If you've been alive long enough, you've probably seen or visited a Starbucks before. And chances are you had a good experience. Starbucks has been inspiring and nurturing the human spirit since it was founded in 1971. At the root of the famous coffee chain is a deep commitment to create a sense of belonging with their customers. This energy is infectious and allows Starbucks to attract and retain top talent while providing exceptional experiences to customers.

Mismanaging diversity and inclusion can be embarrassing... and expensive. Let's discuss the legal ramifications of fumbling the diversity and inclusion ball.

LEGAL RAMIFICATIONS

Although the main reason for fostering a diverse and inclusive culture at work is because it is the right thing to do and it leads to higher levels of performance, it is also important to mention the legal ramifications of not making D&I a focus. By not being aware and intentional with D&I matters, you are making yourself and your organization more susceptible to discrimination, harassment, and other HR-related lawsuits.

Most people have heard of your typical race or gender-based discrimination claims. Situations happen in which one or more employees feel like they were discriminated against as a result of their gender, color of their skin, or ethnicity. However, several other forms of discrimination and bias are worth mentioning. For example, an article released by *Bloomberg* in May of 2019 discussed one of the largest discrimination and bias payouts ever recorded.

JP Morgan Chase & Co. agreed to resolve a discrimination claim by paying a total of $5 million to parents who were affected by their biased parental leave policy. The claim originated from a male employee who was denied the sixteen weeks of leave primary caregivers receive when their child is born. According to the employee's attorneys, the payout was "the biggest recorded settlement in a US parental leave discrimination case."[82]

Unconscious bias, especially at work, can lead to issues such as this parental leave discrimination case. By not treating

---

[82] Stephen Miller, "JPMorgan Chase Settles Paternity Leave Suit over 'Primary Caregiver' for $5 Million," SHRM, August 16, 2019.

parents equal regardless of gender, you can end up in a position as bad, if not worse, as JP Morgan Chase & Co. Although the bank did not officially admit fault in the case, the large settlement suggests there are at least some opportunities for improvement in the inclusivity—or lack thereof—at the company.

Something as simple as assuming fathers are not or should not be considered primary caregivers is problematic. Even though there are no national paid parental leave policies as I'm writing this book, that should not be an excuse for companies not to do the right thing. My recommendation is for companies to allow either parent access to the same amount of parental leave, regardless of gender, whether they are the primary caregiver or not. The focus should be on being fair and consistent while also avoiding legal issues.

Is it possible to focus too much on D&I? The answer to the question is "It depends." The reason being this is a controversial issue, particularly in the United States. Since I do not have a law degree, I do not have the credentials to legally advise you or your organization; however, there are some legal ramifications to not having a diverse and inclusive environment that you should be aware of.

REVERSE DISCRIMINATION

According to an article published in *The Atlantic* titled "The Myth of Reverse Racism" by Vann R. Newkirk II, "Data shows that many Americans do perceive reverse racism to be a significant societal problem. A 2016 Public Religion Research Institute poll indicates that half of all Americans,

57 percent of all white people, and 66 percent of the white working-class, believe that discrimination against white people is as big a problem in America as discrimination against black people."[83] With those statistics in mind, many people who find themselves in the majority would most likely agree that focusing too much on D&I can lead to reverse discrimination.

Newkirk II goes on to state in his article that "Fears of reverse racism fly in the face of data. White students still make up almost three-quarters of all private external scholarship recipients in four-year bachelor's programs, almost two-thirds of all institutional grants and scholarship recipients, and over three-quarters of all merit-based grants and scholarships, although white people only make up about 62 percent of the college student population and about half of all people under 19. White students are more likely than black, Latino, and Asian students to receive scholarships."[84]

The article from *The Atlantic* also states "The usage of 'reverse racism' and 'reverse discrimination' arose in direct response to affirmative and race-based policies in the 1970s. Even as outright quotas and more open attempts to equalize the numbers of minority enrollees were defeated, the term stuck. A 1979 *California Law Review* article defines reverse discrimination as a phenomenon where "individual blacks and members of other minority groups began to be given

83   Vann R. Newkirk II, "How the Myth of Reverse Racism Drives the Affirmative Action Debate," The Atlantic Media Company, August 10, 2017.

84   Ibid.

benefits at the expense of whites who, apart from race, would have had a superior claim to enjoy them."[85]

Clearly, there is a divide between whether affirmative action is valuable or detrimental, even though several data points suggest that affirmative action and other minority-focused initiatives are still needed. How someone in the majority can pull the racism card is hard to comprehend. By definition, racism requires someone of a particular race to believe their race is superior to another. When you have been historically and systematically oppressed, it's hard for someone not in an underrepresented group to make that claim. Reverse racism is essentially a construct that became elevated out of white privilege.

However, it is important to be knowledgeable of both opinions on the matter. Understanding the various components of D&I and reverse discrimination will help you make good decisions.

What is unconscious bias and what role does it play at work?

UNCONSCIOUS BIAS

I would be remiss to discuss discrimination in the workplace without mentioning the mindsets that tend to lead to these issues. Unintentional discrimination issues are not uncommon. Unconscious bias is one of the main culprits when it comes to discrimination issues. According to an article released by The Society of Human Resource

---

85 Ibid.

Management (SHRM) titled "Putting Humanity into HR Compliance: Become Aware of Unconscious Bias," unconscious bias occurs when someone who does not know you makes assumptions about your character, intelligence, or capabilities based on how you look, speak, or behave. This person does so not even knowing he or she is thinking or reacting this way."[86]

Unconscious bias is not always a bad thing either. It helps us filter through the thousands of stimuli we encounter every day in order to make effective decisions. We would take much longer to make decisions if we did not leverage our unconscious bias.

However, the key is to be aware of the negative implications of our unconscious bias.

Staying away from dark alleys at night without having to consciously think about it is one thing, but disregarding a resume due to an applicant's name is another.

The article from the SHRM goes on to state "Unconscious bias in the workplace often manifests in the hiring and promotion process," and "In hiring decisions, people tend to gravitate toward those who are inside our own group. We automatically feel comfortable with people who think like us, act like us, and look like us."[87]

---

86 Jathan Janove, "Putting Humanity into HR Compliance: Become Aware of Unconscious Bias," SHRM, June 5, 2019.
87 Ibid.

So, what you end up having is an organization with subpar levels of diversity and above-average levels of unconscious bias that perpetuates the less than desirable status quo. There is no doubt that people tend to feel most comfortable with people who are similar to them. However, "That subjective comfort, often talked about in terms of 'fit' in a particular workplace culture, overrides what should be an assessment of objective qualifications. In promotions, people also tend to promote those who they think are 'leadership material.' These types of statements are often red flags for unconscious bias as employers make decisions based on assumptions about or stereotypes of traditional leaders—typically older, Caucasian men."[88]

So how can you mitigate your unconscious bias? Camille Olson, a partner at Seyfarth Shaw in Chicago, Illinois, recommends a three-step approach for mitigating unconscious bias. Below are overviews of each step:

1. Recognize the "associations, group loyalties, and stereotypes in order to become more conscious of our potential bias."[89] Perspective-taking is a term used that demonstrates this step. Essentially, you must seek to understand the perspective of someone who is not like you. By taking a moment to pause and reflect on other points of view, you are much more likely to be more inclusive in your decision-making.

2. Leaders must be bought in to the value of mitigating unconscious bias in the workplace especially as it relates

---

88   Ibid.
89   Ibid.

to hiring, disciplinary, and promotion decisions. By utilizing a "structured decision-making protocol," leaders are much more likely to make better business decisions.[90]

3. Lastly, strictly enforced policies and procedures must be implemented within the organization to minimize biased decision-making. "Examples of those structures include hiring checklists, decision-making documentation processes, compensation audits, performance appraisal systems, cultural audits, policy development, and accessibility audits."[91]

NOT DIVERSE ENOUGH

"I have really enjoyed the interview process and I think this would be a great company to work for; however, I do not see anybody who looks like me in senior leadership. Unfortunately, that is very important to me, so I have decided to accept another offer at a company with more women in leadership."

This is a response a company I consulted for received after offering a highly talented woman a job at their company. Luckily, after months of D&I consulting, I was able to assist the organization with improving their D&I efforts. Many companies deal with similar issues like the one previously mentioned. At least the company I was consulting for was aware of its shortcomings and brought me on board specifically to address those opportunities.

---

90 Ibid.
91 Eddie Kim, "What the Courts Make of 'Reverse Discrimination' Complaints," Accessed May 20, 2020.

Many companies are not aware of their lack of D&I. Other companies are aware and do not take appropriate action to fix the issue. Some companies are aware, attempt to take action, but don't yield positive results for a variety of reasons. The key to any D&I strategy is to first understand why D&I is important.

D&I is about obtaining diversity of thought.

When you have diversity of thought on a team, you have a much more representative mentality of the world, as well as your clients.

People who have different backgrounds, personality styles, sexual orientations, genders, ages, etc. help to provide a variety of perspectives that can add tremendous value. Studies have shown that having diverse people on a team solving problems leads to higher performance. Diverse and inclusive companies have also proven to have better recruitment and retention results than companies that are less diverse and inclusive. So how can organizations and senior leaders foster an environment of diversity and inclusion? In order to answer that question, we must first determine what underrepresented groups want.

WHAT UNDERREPRESENTED GROUPS WANT

In order to truly appeal to people in underrepresented groups, you must understand their struggles and what they value. According to an article titled "Survey: What Diversity and Inclusion Policies Do Employees Actually Want?" by Matt

Krentz, he believes women, minorities, and the LGBTQ community want the following:[92]

Women
- Career and family flexibility
- Visible role models in the leadership team

Minorities (Racial and Ethnic)
- Clear pathway for advancement
- Senior leaders who look like them

LGBTQ
- Want inclusive environment
- Ability to feel like they can be their authentic selves

As a leader, if you are aware of what your target candidates want, you can better prepare to deliver on their wants and needs. In addition to the items listed above, you can effectively target D&I by focusing on leadership commitment, anti-discrimination policies, effective training, and measuring key performance indicators (KPIs).

Goal Setting · Employee Surveys · Brainstorming · Implementation · Follow Up · Repeat?

D&I ROADMAP
So how do you correctly implement a D&I strategy? The answer is: very intentionally and patiently. The initiative

92 Matt Krentz, "Survey: What Diversity and Inclusion Policies Do Employees Actually Want?" Harvard Business Review, February 5, 2019.

must be well thought out and have a long-term approach aligned with company strategy. People do not typically handle change well, so you have to ease into making changes in philosophy and organizational culture.

Below is a roadmap that I take my clients through when I do D&I consulting as well as typical timeframes for each step:

Step 1. Goal Setting (1–2 months)
In the Goal Setting phase, I walk clients through the process of creating two to three D&I goals for the next three to five years. I also assist with the creation of D&I employee talking points to share goals with the team.

Example Goal: Hire a workforce that mirrors the diverse clientele you serve. For example, if your clients are 70 percent female and 30 percent male, you should strive for your team to have a similar makeup.

Step 2. Employee Surveys (1–3 months)
In the Employee Surveys phase, I help clients create and administer employee surveys designed to solicit feedback, ideas, etc. regarding D&I. The surveys are also used to gather personal data from existing employees if not already on file. This data helps classify existing team members based on what underrepresented groups they may fall in.

Step 3. Brainstorming (2–4 months)
In the Brainstorming phase, I review feedback from the surveys along with the leadership team and determine a plan of action based on survey results. The goal is to finalize at least two or three D&I goals for the next three to five years by the conclusion of this step. Additionally, strategic planning for complete integration and execution of D&I strategy occurs during this phase of the road map. Official D&I talking points should be drafted for employee communication, marketing, and recruitment purposes.

Step 4. Implementation (3–6 months)
In the Implementation phase, a D&I committee should be created. The committee should include various levels of employees to have a well-rounded group. The establishment of relationships with organizations within each of the underrepresented groups: women, LGBTQ, and minorities (Racial and Ethnic), etc. should also take place during this step. It is important to note that there are more underrepresented groups than the three previously listed. Each company is different and should determine which groups they would like to target first based on their market, current workforce, and client base, but all underrepresented groups deserve your attention.

Training should be administered to existing employees as well as new hires to ensure employees are removing bias, increasing cultural competency, and not undervaluing the needs of individuals in underrepresented groups. Clear and consistently enforced anti-discrimination policies should be rolled out to the team and bias should be removed from evaluation and promotion decisions. Lastly, senior leadership must show support of D&I goals and initiatives.

Step 5. Follow Up (once steps 1–4 are completed)
Once steps 1–4 are completed, it is important to track D&I performance and review during performance evaluations. Employee surveys should be sent out at least once a year to track progress. Moreover, promotion and pay across diversity cohorts should be measured and other metrics should be identified as KPIs. I typically recommend utilizing retention, morale/engagement, and productivity as ways to measure the impact of a D&I strategy.

Step 6. Repeat (If needed)
After step five of the D&I roadmap, hopefully, there are only minor tweaks that need to be made to the initiative if any. However, if there are still major issues with D&I progress by the time we get to this phase, we should consider starting the road map over again.

Now that we have defined D&I, explored the legal ramifications of various initiatives or lack thereof, and provided a roadmap for a successful implementation of D&I into your culture, let's summarize what we have learned.

***

D&I IN A NUTSHELL

The goal of any D&I initiative should be to obtain diversity of thought. Statistics show that higher levels of performance are associated with firms that have more inclusive and diverse workforces. Aside from company performance, focusing on D&I can lead to better retention, productivity, and a decreased chance of facing a discrimination lawsuit. Be aware of opposition to D&I initiatives such as affirmative action. Additionally, reverse discrimination is something that must be considered as you work to improve D&I at your organization. I encourage senior leaders to be patient and intentional with implementing a D&I strategy. D&I should be integrated within company culture and should be a long-term focus in order to be successful.

CONTEXT

Let's take a moment to debrief what we have learned so far. An award-winning culture can be fostered by a compelling purpose and excellent people. After diving into the positives of culture, we provided a roadmap for establishing your "why." An inspiring purpose helps attract talent and retain talent. The hiring process should be taken very seriously. Patience and intentionality will help you make good hiring decisions.

Cultures that promote diversity and inclusion have proven to lead to higher levels of performance. To obtain a competitive advantage through your people, it is important to seek diversity of thought when hiring. By following my diversity and inclusion road map, you will be able to create an initiative that aligns with your overall company strategy. Remember to think through unconscious bias and how that influences behavior. By understanding the barriers of a culture centered around diversity and inclusion, you will be better positioned to overcome those barriers.

ACTIVITY:

1. Why do you think having a diverse and inclusive workforce leads to better organizational performance?
2. If you were a Chief D&I officer, how would you make sure your organization created an inclusive environment for all team members?
3. Many people believe you have to sacrifice quality in order to improve diversity. How would you respond to a member of your senior leadership team if they said that?

Picture This: The "People" portion of The Circle of Leadership framework is not complete without having a diverse and inclusive organization. This should be a priority when hiring and looking to create an engaging workplace culture.

CHAPTER 7:

RETENTION (THE ART OF APPRECIATION)

"If managers cannot see beyond what their employees are doing and help them understand who they are helping and how they are making a difference, then those jobs are bound to be miserable."

–PATRICK LENCIONI

***

WHY RECOGNITION MATTERS

When you're the CEO of one of the largest food companies, chances are you've encountered a plethora of different leadership scenarios. This was certainly the case for David Novak. David was formerly the CEO of Yum! Brands, Inc. where he led thousands of restaurants in over one hundred countries across the world.[93] Despite the magnitude of responsibility

---

93   "David Novak," David Novak Leadership, Accessed May 22, 2020.

that came with this role, one of David's most memorable lessons in leadership did not come from his time at Yum! Brands, Inc.

In episode "#188" of *The Entreleadership Podcast*, David talked about the power of recognition and why it matters. When David was in charge of operations at Pepsi, he would often host what he called round-table discussions in the distribution centers. During a discussion at a facility in St. Louis, Missouri, David recalled asking a group of salesmen who was the best when it came to merchandising. Without hesitation, the group began to talk about a guy named Bob and how he was the best merchandiser in the company.

According to David, "He taught me more in five hours than I learned my first three years."[94] By the end of David's time with the group, he noticed Bob was crying as everyone was singing his praises. When David realized Bob was crying, he quickly asked him what was wrong. Bob responded by saying, "I've been in this company for forty-seven years. I'm retiring in two weeks, and I didn't know people felt this way about me." From that day on, David made a commitment to make sure that "the Bobs in the world are really recognized for what they do."[95]

Unfortunately, there are stories similar to Bob's all over the world. You may know a Bob or maybe you are Bob! Either way, I challenge you to make a vow. Vow that you will make sure people like Bob receive the recognition they deserve.

---

94 Coleman, Ken. "#188: David Novak—Why Recognition Matters". Podcast. The Entreleadership Podcast, 2017.

95 Ibid.

There are Bobs everywhere, and as their leader, it's your job to let them know you care.

RECOGNITION DEFICIT

According to David, there is what he refers to as a "recognition deficit."[96] A "recognition deficit" is a significant shortage of genuine and timely recognition given to team members by their leaders. During the podcast interview, David shared that "Almost 85 percent of people feel like their supervisor doesn't recognize them for what they do."[97] This is obviously a huge problem and certainly plays a role in employee turnover and engagement.

In order to get the ball rolling, try to catch your team doing things right. We have a tendency as leaders to only point out the bad, but it is equally important to point out the good. This does not mean you do not address poor performance because you absolutely have to. Try to make a concerted effort to spontaneously, yet consistently, recognize your people.

The story of Bob is one that all leaders should try to eliminate in their organizations. Luckily, solving any problem begins with awareness. Now that you are aware of the "recognition deficit" out in the world today, it is your job to fix it. Below are two of the biggest reasons why there is such a "recognition deficit" according to David:[98]

---

96   Ibid.
97   Ibid.
98   Ibid.

1. Supervisors are afraid to recognize their people because if they do, they will stop working as hard
2. People feel like if one person gets recognized, others will want to be recognized as well
3. Neither of these reasons justifies not recognizing and appreciating your people. David shared that "60 percent of people will tell you that they are as motivated from recognition as they are from making money." In fact, according to David, employees state that they would work harder if they were recognized. In my experience, I have found that to be true as well.[99]

Ultimately, leaders need to be coaches and provide consistent and genuine appreciation. By creating a culture of recognizing your team, you are more likely to have a strong relationship with your team and retain your good performers. Let's take a look at some of the more nuanced ways of focusing on employee retention. Guess what it starts with? Appreciation.

---

99 Ibid.

THE ART OF APPRECIATION

The first step in any company's plan to retain their employees should be to focus on appreciation. I can speak from personal experience when I say that when you do not feel appreciated, you are much more likely to seek other job opportunities. People want to be acknowledged for their contributions. Appreciation must be genuine, and you must be intentional with showcasing it to your team. The art of appreciation can vary on how it is executed but the goal remains to show your employees that you value, hear, and see them.

Author Kristie Rogers wrote an article released in *The Harvard Business Review* titled "Do Your Employees Feel Respected?" In that article, Rogers states "According to a McKinsey global survey of more than 1,000 executives, managers, and employees, praise from an immediate manager, attention from a leader, and opportunities to head a project have more impact on motivation than do monetary incentives."[100]

People want more than just fair pay at work; they want to feel respected and valued. The question we should be asking ourselves is how? Below are eight ways you can inspire and recognize your team:

---

100 Kristie Rogers, "Do Your Employees Feel Respected?" Harvard Business Review, June 21, 2018.

EIGHT WAYS TO INSPIRE AND RECOGNIZE YOUR TEAM

1. Time off

Work/life balance is crucial for employees to perform at their best. Nobody wants to spend all of their time at work, so show your team that you appreciate them by giving them a day off. Even cutting the workday short on a Friday could have a significant impact. Who wouldn't like to start their weekend on Friday after lunch?

2. Handwritten cards (Thank You, Birthday, Anniversary, etc.)

Remembering the names of family members and significant others can have a tremendous impact on your team. The same goes for dates and events such as birthdays and anniversaries. Show how much you care about your employees by giving them handwritten notes. Your effort and intentionality will not go unnoticed.

3. Team building events/activities

Show your appreciation to your team by planning a non-work-related group activity. Not only will this allow your team to bond outside of work, it is a fun way to connect with your team and strengthen teamwork. Activities such as bowling, golfing, or going out to dinner could do the trick. Even a virtual happy hour could loosen up your team and allow everyone to build stronger relationships with each other.

4. Free food

Most people love food… especially if it's free. Put this theory to the test by purchasing donuts and coffee in the morning for your team or getting food catered for lunch. You'll be surprised by how well your team might respond to a good free meal.

5. Cash

Cold hard cash is still very valuable to people. Your employees are no different. Send them fifty dollars to use on date night with their spouse and see how they react. You'll probably be one of the only leaders who have done anything remotely close to that.

6. Public acknowledgment/recognition

What's better than recognition? Public recognition. Acknowledging your team in front of their peers can go a long way. The next time you want to acknowledge someone, do it at a team meeting so they can feel special. If you know for a fact someone on your team would not like being recognized in front of others, feel free to do it individually instead. Know your team and do what will have the biggest impact on them.

7. Be consistent

To have a long-term impact on your team, you should try to be as consistent as possible with inspiring your team. It's easy to recognize your team occasionally; it's much more difficult to incorporate recognition into your company culture. Showing gratitude should be the norm. Carve out time during all meetings to give kudos to each other and watch how people light up when they're recognized.

8. Be genuine

Arguably most important of all, be genuine! People will realize if you are not being authentic, and that is the only thing worse than not recognizing your people at all.

Appreciation should be part of your organization's compensation plan.

People do not only work for money; they work for significance and to feel valued. It should, therefore, be your priority to be genuine in expressing gratitude toward your team. Try to highlight things you truly appreciate about your team and their performance but put thought into it, so it does not come across as insincere.

IMPROVING EMPLOYEE RETENTION

From a business perspective, appreciating and recognizing your people decreases turnover and improves employee engagement. According to Mercer, "More than one-third of Americans are actively looking for a new job, with 43 percent citing lack of recognition as one of the main reasons for their unhappiness."[101] With this large of your workforce potentially looking for a new job, what things can you do to improve employee retention?

Below is a road map you can follow step by step to get your organization back on track:

1. Improve Hiring and Onboarding Process
The first thing you need to do to improve retention is to take more time to get to know your applicants so you can make better hiring decisions. Too often we are in a crunch for

---

101 "10 Easy Ways to Recognize Your Team," EntreLeadership, December 10, 2017.

staffing and make poor decisions when hiring. If you hire better candidates to begin with, you will set yourself up to retain your employees because they will be a good fit for your organization. Slow down, get to know your applicants, and use a standardized approach to the interview process so you can evaluate each applicant adequately.

Once you've selected the right candidate, make sure you put effort into making the onboarding process a positive experience. Be prepared for the candidate's orientation. Have your materials ready and remember that you can only make a first impression once! Do your best to make orientation day memorable in a good way. Make your new hires feel special, not only on orientation day but every day.

2. Thirty, Sixty, and Ninety-day Check-ins
I cannot tell you the number of times I have heard from a new hire that they were unhappy with the job. In those situations, I typically find that what they are needing are simple fixes. However, my managers that did not conduct thirty, sixty, and ninety-day check-ins often missed out on the opportunity to gain that information in a timely manner. Do not let too much time pass by before seeing how your new hires are doing. Something as simple as addressing a scheduling concern or training opportunity can be the difference between losing an employee or keeping them.

Be sure to be structured and consistent with the questions asked during these check-ins. Making the new hires feel comfortable voicing any concerns and taking them seriously is also important for managers to do. I recommend at least asking what they've enjoyed most and least about the job and company so far. I would also encourage leaders to ask specifically what they can do to make the job more enjoyable. Thirty, sixty, and ninety-day check-ins are also a great opportunity to give feedback, and hopefully, praise.

3. Provide Adequate Training

People want to feel like they are doing well at work. I find that most people do not intentionally try to perform poorly. However, employees need to be trained effectively to be competent at their job. Make sure that you have clearly articulated expectations for your new employee and that you train them to be able to successfully perform their job responsibilities. You never want an employee who is struggling to say they are not performing well due to a lack of proper training.

Training should be a combination of shadowing a competent performer, on the job training, close supervision by a trainer, and anything else a new hire needs to be successful. It's also important to note that employees may need to be re-trained on certain tasks. Not only if there is a new rollout but also to make sure people are being as efficient as possible. Proper training also allows you to delegate, supervise, and hold employees accountable. You cannot go through The Circle of Leadership framework without proper training.

Roughly one-third of new hires quit their job after six months, so there is no debating the value that a well-executed thirty, sixty, ninety-day process and adequate training can provide.[102,103]

4. Offer Retention Bonuses

Incentives can be an effective motivator when administered correctly. It's important to note that creativity might be hindered by standard "if/then" awards (i.e., if you achieve x, then you get y). However, try giving bonuses to leaders for retaining top talent. If you define the tasks that lead to retention and make leaders have a narrow focus toward it, incentives might be just the motivation a leader needs to take retention seriously.

Be cautious of managers not terminating poor performing employees because of focusing on retention. You want to employ the best, retain the best, and get rid of the rest. This does not mean terminate every employee who is not your best, but it does mean to let go of your poor performers.

Be flexible with accommodating employees and their needs. If you can help make life easier for them, try your best to do so. Make sure your employees feel like they are heard. If you invest in your team, they will invest in your organization and the clients you serve. Reward leaders for minimizing turnover in their area. Turnover can be costly, so providing a bonus is the least you can do for your leaders saving the company money and talent.

---

102 Marcel Schwantes, "The Surprising Reason Why So Many Employees Quit Within the First 6 Months," Inc., July 25, 2019.

103 Benjamin Snyder, "Half of Us Have Quit Our Job Because of a Bad Boss," Fortune, April 2, 2015.

According to Total Rewards Solutions, a compensation and benefits firm, organizations should utilize an 80-50-20 rule for performance thresholds. The concept suggests that the minimum threshold should be achievable roughly 80 percent of the time, target performance should be achievable 50 percent of the time, and the maximum performance should be achievable 20 percent of the time.[104] This principle should apply to bonuses of all sorts, in this case, for retention bonuses.

THE TRUTH ABOUT EMPLOYEE ENGAGEMENT

Organizations are anxiously trying to determine how to have a more engaged workforce. It has been proven, that firms with higher levels of employee engagement are more profitable than those with lower levels of employee engagement. However, companies often miss the mark when it comes to improving engagement with their employees. "Disengaged managers cost the US economy $319-$398 Billion annually" and "50 percent of adults have left a job to get away from their manager."[105]

Some think simply increasing wages will lead to more engaged employees. Others believe more perks or a better benefits package will do the trick. Some will send survey after survey just magically hoping for better results. The truth of the matter is too many people are not engaged at work, and companies are literally losing money by the minute in unproductive, non-engaged employees.

---

104 Total Solutions, Accessed May 22, 2020.
105 Benjamin Snyder, "Half of Us Have Quit Our Job Because of a Bad Boss," Fortune, April 2, 2015.

Patrick Lencioni is an author, consultant, and President of The Table Group. Patrick is an expert in leadership, teamwork, and organizational health. In his book titled *The Truth About Employee Engagement*, Patrick shares "a fable about addressing the three root causes of job misery."[106] Patrick tells the story of a retired CEO named Brian Bailey who re-enters the workforce after a short-lived retirement. After Brian discovers that he cannot go very long without managing people and solving problems, he begins testing a theory that he believes can create more employee engagement at work.

In order to understand the theory proposed in the book, it is important to first review the three root causes of what Patrick refers to as misery. Below is a summary of each component:

1. Anonymity
   — "People cannot be fulfilled in their work if they are not known. All human beings need to be understood and appreciated for their unique qualities by someone in a position of authority. People who see themselves as invisible, generic, or anonymous cannot love their jobs, no matter what they are doing."
2. Irrelevance
   — "Everyone needs to know that their job matters to someone. Anyone. Without seeing a connection between the work and the satisfaction of another person or group of people, an employee simply will not find lasting fulfillment. Even the most cynical

---

106 "Patrick Lencioni: The Table Group," The Table Group, Accessed May 22, 2020.

employees need to know that their work matters to someone, even if it's just the boss."

3. Measurement
   — "Employees need to be able to gauge their progress and level of contribution for themselves. They cannot be fulfilled in their work if their success depends on the opinions or whims of another person, no matter how benevolent that person may be. Without a tangible means for assessing success or failure, motivation eventually deteriorates as people see themselves as unable to control their own fate."[107]

Although the three causes of misery seem very simple, they are often not addressed with the intensity they deserve. The benefits of building a culture of engagement are clear and attractive: improved productivity, lower turnover, and higher employee morale. By aggressively attacking the three root causes of misery, organizations will be able to minimize expenses and differentiate themselves in the industry.

There are a few other major benefits to improving employee engagement that Patrick highlights in the book. Below is a list of those benefits:[108]

- Improved sense of ownership among employees
- Attract higher caliber applicants
- Greater sense of teamwork

---

107 Patrick Lencioni, *The Truth about Employee Engagement: A Fable about Addressing the Three Root Causes of Job Misery*, San Francisco, CA: Jossey-Bass & Pfeiffer, 2016.
108 Ibid.

One question that Patrick recommends all companies ask their employees is "What is making you even consider leaving in the first place?"[109] By asking this question, you are proactively addressing reasons why an employee might leave the organization. This is a great way to gather feedback long before an exit interview.

Patrick encourages leaders to get to know their people and goes as far as saying "To manage another human being effectively requires some degree of empathy and curiosity about why that person gets out of bed in the morning, what is on their mind, and how you can contribute to them becoming a better person."[110] This was the exact approach I took toward a former employee who is what I would consider the "most valuable asset."

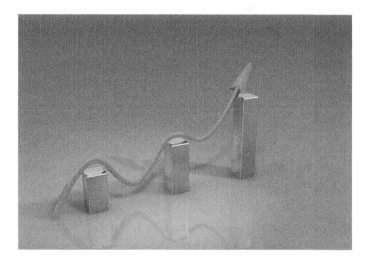

109 Ibid.
110 Ibid.

MOST VALUABLE ASSET (MVA)

I once had a manager who I viewed as a rising star. At the time I started working with her, she was probably in the top fifteen store managers in our division out of approximately ninety retail stores. Although she was very talented, she approached me one day with concerns about her future with the company. She was strongly considering moving on from the organization.

When I asked her why, she stated that she no longer felt challenged and felt like she was not appreciated for the work she had done. After asking several follow-up questions, I also found out that the only family she had was moving over an hour north of where she currently lived, and she wanted to be closer to them.

Fortunately, we were able to outline some challenging goals for her that included training new interns, store managers, and district managers, as well as getting her involved with remodeling projects. We also promised to move her to a location closer to her family once a store became available. I was very transparent about what things she needed to improve in order to be considered a top store manager in the division and win the Store Manager of The Year award. Long story short, not only were we able to retain that manager, she ultimately won the next year's Store Manager of The Year award!

After almost a decade of leading people, I've learned the simple fact that people want to feel valued. In my experience, the number one reason people leave a company is due to a lack of growth in one way, shape, or form. I've also discovered that the number one reason people seek another job is due to the growth opportunity available at a particular company. The truth in the matter is leaders must focus a large portion of their time and energy into their people. If you view your people as your most valuable asset (MVA), they will feel appreciated and valued.

The benefits of fostering an environment of growth are increased engagement, motivation, and retention at work. I once heard that the average cost of turnover is roughly two times an employee's yearly salary. Think about the wasted time, energy, and money every time an employee leaves your organization. Engagement goes hand in hand with motivation. Motivated employees are typically employees who feel valued and challenged at work. A competitive advantage can be formed when your organization has excellent retention through engaging and motivating your team.

Had I not displayed empathy and curiosity with my former store manager who was considering resigning, she would have left the company and for good reason. Through asking the right questions and actively listening, I was able to understand what motivated her and act upon that information. If I can do this, so can you. You just need to be intentional.

***

RETENTION SUMMARY
Everything from placing all employees on the same bonus plan to making work challenging and engaging can minimize turnover. However, the simplest and most cost-effective way to retain your people is to acknowledge them. If you

recognize your employees, you will make work fun. You'd be surprised how many people seek enjoyable work environments even more than money.

> You've created an excellent work environment if people feel like they have the opportunity to do what they do best every day.

Focusing on appreciating your employees will fuel performance and improve retention. People's strengths generate their highest performance today and the greatest improvement in their performance tomorrow.

CONTEXT

Let's take a moment to debrief what we have learned so far. Great culture starts with great people and a compelling purpose. An inspiring vision for the future helps attract talent and retain talent. A diverse workforce is a winning workforce. People who come from different backgrounds are able to leverage a variety of experiences for the sake of good decision-making.

Your people are your most valuable assets (MVA) and should be treated as such. Turnover is expensive and should be avoided unless you are dealing with poor performers. Getting rid of people who are not meeting expectations is considered good turnover. There are several ways you can inspire your team by expressing appreciation. The key is to simply take action and do it.

ACTIVITY:

1. Why do you think turnover is so expensive for an organization?

2. What would you do to improve retention at your organization if turnover was high?

3. Why do you think most people leave organizations? What can be done to solve that problem?

Picture This: Building a culture of valuing your employees begins with improving the hiring and onboarding process, periodically checking in with team members, providing adequate training, and offering incentives to encourage retention. This chapter concludes the "People" portion of The Circle of Leadership framework.

PART 3:

PROCESS

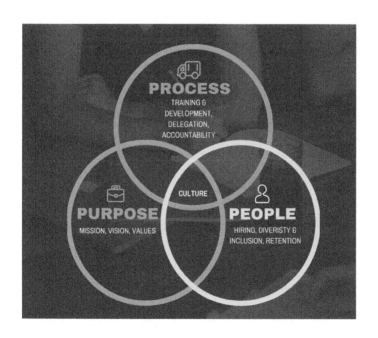

CHAPTER 8:

TRAINING AND DEVELOPMENT

"It doesn't make sense to hire smart people and tell them what to do; we hire smart people so they can tell us what to do."

−STEVE JOBS

***

PERFECT PRACTICE

"How did you get so good at having tough conversations?" I couldn't help but laugh in response to my intern's question. As she witnessed me terminating an employee, I couldn't help but reminisce about all the times I planned to have a flawlessly executed tough conversation only for it to end up going terribly wrong. After reflecting on the question my intern asked me, I realized that the answer was "perfect practice." Practice alone does not make you perfect—practicing perfectly, or as close to perfect as possible, does. How do you make sure you are practicing to perfection? The answer is to have the right teacher and the right attitude.

During my first internship with an international grocery company, I was paired with a seasoned district manager named Charles. Charles was very friendly, charismatic, and easy to talk to. However, Charles was also very tough on his trainees and interns. I was no exception. I remember him telling me on my first day that I should take notes as if I had to do the task on my own the very next time. He promised to answer any of my questions during the note-taking process but challenged me to ask enough detailed questions to feel comfortable doing it alone afterward.

Charles was a man of his word and put my note-taking skills to the test during our next store visit. As we arrived at our second store for the day, he told me that I would be handling all the tasks for the visit. As I stumbled through my notes, I quickly realized how poorly of a job I did with asking him questions. When I asked Charles what to do during a store financial audit, he replied, "I don't know, what does it say in your notes?"

Although Charles's approach was a little harsh, I learned more from Charles than I did any other district manager I trained with. I went on to get a full-time job offer after my internship, so I think it's safe to say Charles was an effective trainer. Charles challenged you to bring your "A-game" every day and practice as close to perfect as possible. He also forced you to think critically and make decisions. But he provided the space for you to fail in order for you to learn and grow. That is precisely what I did specifically during my time training with Charles. Charles is still one of my mentors to this day. I learned the value of asking the right questions and striving to practice perfectly—or at least attempting to—that summer, and those are two principles that I continue to live by.

Nobody is successful on their own. We all have coaches, teachers, trainers, and mentors that have had an impact on our lives. Without proper guidance, it is difficult to reach our full potential. Because of my ability to watch successful people such as Charles handle a variety of tough personnel issues, I was able to learn how to approach them. I've also learned from experience that even if you observe the proper way to do something, that doesn't mean you will be able to execute it correctly alone.

Everyone learns differently, and therefore you should include a multitude of approaches to training. I would recommend a combination of showing someone how to do something, shadowing them doing it while providing feedback, and letting them perform tasks independently with occasional follow up. Utilizing various approaches will help people learn regardless of if they are a visual, verbal, or hands-on learner.

Now that storytime is over, let's take a deep dive into the nuts and bolts of training and development.

EMPLOYEE DEVELOPMENT

HR strategies and initiatives should be given three-year cycles if possible—meaning if you are not thinking at least three years into the future when contemplating HR decisions, you are not thinking long-term enough. This surprises many leaders especially in the "I want it now" world we live in today. Leaders need to think strategically, especially when it comes to their people and processes. Part of your human capital strategy should revolve around training and employee development.

Employee development begins during the selection process. You've got to ask the right questions so you can select the right candidate. This is more than half the battle when it comes to successfully training and retaining employees. The next leg in employee development is the new hire orientation or onboarding. Understanding your employees' career goals is important. Once you understand the long-term goals of your people, you can better assist them in reaching those goals. You want to talk about the future with your employees early and often. The onboarding process is a great place to drive that message home.

Once you've successfully completed onboarding, your focus as a leader should be training. I like to think of the training process as boot camp. Training should stretch the new hire but not break them. You should show support and empathy toward your new hires but challenge them at the same time.

Leaders often think the only time you train is when you have new people on your team. This could not be further from the truth. All employees should be continuously challenged. One way to do that is by re-training employees on best practices for performing their job. Time spent on training is a wise return on investment when executed properly. Anytime you are focusing on growing your team, you will reap dividends as a result.

Talent management is the last step in the employee development process. Constant feedback and guidance should be given throughout an employee's career to best manage their performance. Sometimes talent management leads to employee growth, other times it leads to what one of my former managers would call "a promotion to customer" which we will discuss later in the book in the accountability chapter.

TRAINING DESIGN PROCESS

Designing your training deserves your undivided attention due to the array of options that you are privy to. While studying for my Master of Science degree in Management, Strategy, and Leadership, I came across a book during one of my HR classes that had a profound impact on how I view training and development. The following content comes from that expert resource. According to *Employee Training & Development* (7th edition) by Raymond A. Noe, the training design process consists of seven major steps.[111] The outline of the steps is listed below:

1. Conducting needs assessment
   — Awareness is key when designing your organization's training process. Step 1 should consist of taking inventory of your current needs. This should be done through the lens of the organization, your team,

---

111 Raymond A. Noe, *Employee Training and Development*, New York, NY: McGraw-Hill Education, 2020.

and based on an analysis of the tasks performed in the various roles.

2. Ensuring employees' readiness for training
   — Even the best strategy and action plan can fail if your team is not prepared for the changes. It is vital to assess the attitudes and motivation of your team especially around the basic skills that you're looking to focus on.

3. Creating a learning environment
   — Once you are aware of the needs of your organization and team and have adequately ensured your people are ready for training, it is time to set the stage for training to take place. This step entails mapping out clear learning objectives, providing meaningful material to your team, practicing and providing feedback, fostering an environment of learning, leading by example through modeling, and ensuring you are administratively ready for execution.

4. Ensuring transfer of training
   — To ensure training sticks, it is important to practice self-management and create a culture where peer and manager support is commonplace.

5. Developing an evaluation plan
   — Follow up is crucial for a training process to work. So, taking time to proactively think through what the feedback process will look like is important. Develop an evaluation plan by identifying intended learning outcomes, solidifying evaluation design, and conducting a plan cost-benefit analysis.

6. Selecting a training method
   — You can have good intent with designing a training process and it still not be effective. One way to

increase the likelihood of success is to spend time thinking through training methods. What would work best for your team and organization? A traditional approach? E-learning? Combination of both? These are questions that must be answered.

7. Monitoring and evaluating the program
   — If you roll something out, you must follow up on the execution of that plan. Check and adjust is something you should be doing early and often. Conduct evaluations at pre-determined timeframes but feel free to make decisions outside of that timeframe if needed. Continuous improvement should be the aim.

The ultimate goal of designing a training process should be a successfully trained employee. In order to accomplish that, you must know what the needs of the job entail so you can adequately prepare new hires for their roles. You want to ensure new hires can learn in the environment you create and are able to receive feedback on how they are doing. One of the key lessons in training and development can be found in the intense training process to become a United States Navy fighter pilot. Let's discuss why.

EARN YOUR WINGS

Navy fighter pilots are some of the most courageous human beings on earth. The composure and competence required for these pilots to do their job are remarkable. The precision and accuracy that comes with the job requires a significant amount of time and practice. In fact, the Navy fighter pilot training process takes roughly two years and often requires pilots to be on multiple flights per day.

Constant evaluation, incremental increases in responsibility, and hours of relentless preparation are expected during training. The training process is so arduous that over 50 percent of people drop out of the program. The Navy wants to make sure that all their pilots "earn their wings." The perfect practice involved with the training process is a large reason why Navy fighter pilots can perform their job so well. The constant training and pressure produce excellence. You not only have to select the right person first, but you've got to give them the tools and resources to be successful once you bring them on board.

I can remember back to my high school football days when we had two practices a day in the summertime, a.k.a. "Two-A-Days." Any football player will tell you that Two-A-Days are not easy. Not only are you putting your mind and body under extreme pressure, you're doing so in the sweltering heat of peak summertime... twice a day!

Two-A-Days are where you learn the plays, understand the team philosophy, and sharpen your game. It's also a time to prepare. If you can power through Two-A-Days and come out stronger than you were when you started, the season should be a piece of cake. The phase of preparation was the foundation of our confidence when the season started. When you know you've put the work in, you are already successful.

This is the same approach leaders should take with training. Put the work in upfront to select the right person for the job and then invest in training so that person can win. Let's look deeper into how to effectively manage talent once they have successfully completed the initial training program.

TALENT MANAGEMENT

According to Michigan State University's Master of Science Talent Management and Development course, talent management is "a continuous process that plans talent needs, builds an image to attract the very best, ensures that new hires are immediately productive, helps to retain the very best, and facilitates the continuous movement of talent to where it can have the most impact within the organization."[112]

Talent management is all about getting the most out of your people. An effective talent management initiative should "drive short- and long-term results by building culture."[113]

In addition to increasing the productivity of your human talent, talent management can also help your organization achieve a competitive advantage. If you perfect the way to optimize recruiting, retain top talent, and get the most out of your people, you will better leverage your most important assets—your people. Having a distinct talent management program is a way for organizations to further distinguish themselves from their competitors, which will improve recruitment and retention efforts.

---

112 Tyler Smeltekop, "The Michigan State University Course Materials Program: Packing Up Your Textbook Troubles with Course Packs," Against the Grain 26, no. 5 (2014): 11.

113 Ibid.

So, what we've covered so far probably doesn't surprise you. Prioritize your people and invest in their training. Got it. It's not rocket science, right? But leaders fail at accomplishing this every day. Take note of the following tenants of talent management to equip yourself with what it takes to succeed at talent management.

THREE TENANTS OF TALENT MANAGEMENT

There are several definitions and components of talent management. Below are my three tenants of talent management based on my experience and the research I've done. This unique approach to talent development will help you create an award-winning program.

1. Align talent development strategy with overall business goals including mission, vision, and values.
2. Focus on purpose, people, and processes to drive results.
3. Hold leaders accountable by measuring KPIs such as productivity, engagement, and retention.

Integrating practices across all business functions is essential for talent management to reach its potential. Below is a model found in Michigan State University's Master of Science Talent and Management course:

INTEGRATED TALENT MANAGEMENT

1. Prepare for the future (Develop)
2. Build a strong team (Engage)
3. Enable performance (Align)
4. Reward performance (Develop)

The four parts of their talent management model help you to attract, engage, develop, and retain your workforce. Improvement tends to happen when progress gets measured. Be sure to track progress and communicate small wins to your team to gather momentum. Integrating talent management with HR initiatives is especially important for synergy across all human capital initiatives.

Not all companies that focus on talent management are successful. Organizations often fail due to a few crucial missteps which are listed below:

- Not selecting the right candidate
- Not being proactive
- Not thinking long term

Proper planning leads to much better execution. The same holds true for talent management initiatives. Challenges will arise regardless of the amount of time spent preparing, however, you are much more likely to overcome barriers when you plan ahead.

There are some intangibles to performance that must be considered when discussing training and development. Luckily, a famous author discovered an equation to address this.

PERFORMANCE FORMULA

On episode ninety-six of *The Entreleadership Podcast*, host Ken Coleman interviewed the son of the legendary Zig Ziglar, Tom Ziglar. Tom is the CEO of The Zig Ziglar Corporation, which has been in business for over forty years.

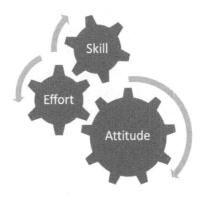

In the episode, Tom explains what he refers to as the "performance equation." The performance equation is A times E times S equals P. The A stands for attitude, the E stands for effort, the S stands for skill, and the P stands for performance. Tom goes on to explain how people do not buy training—they buy the results of what training provides. Ultimately, organizations want to improve performance and that can be accomplished by focusing on attitude, effort, and skills.

Tom went on to share a few stories that articulate the appropriate mindset one should have in regard to attitude. Tom recalled checking in to an airport in Phoenix, Arizona when he was a teenager. Tom's dad was told by the agents that his flight was delayed for hours. In response to the agent, he looked at the guy and said "Fantastic!" When the agent asked Tom's dad what he meant by it he said, "Well, you know there's only three reasons why it could be delayed. The weather's bad, the equipment's bad, or the flight crew is not here. You know, there's something wrong, and if any three of those reasons are going on, I don't want to be up there in the air. I want to be right here on the ground. That's good. Fantastic."[114]

Tom was explaining the impact that a positive attitude can have on yourself and those around you. Having the right mindset can amplify your performance by serving as a multiplier to your effort and skill.

TOM ZIGLAR

Zig Ziglar was a salesmen, motivational speaker, and author among other titles. One of Zig's famous quotes is: "You are what you are and where you are because of what goes into your mind." Tom explained in his podcast interview that "you can change what you are and where you are by changing what goes into your mind, or being simpler I've changed it this way, I said what you feed your mind determines your appetite. In other words, what goes in is going to determine what you desire."[115]

Tom shared a short story about a time he shared those thoughts at a conference. In response to Tom sharing his perspective, a lady stood up in the back of the room and said, "That's just like NASCAR." Slightly confused, Tom asked the lady, "How is it like NASCAR?" In other words, "How does what you feed your mind determine your appetite like NASCAR?" Tom then stated that her response was "It's simple. When you're going around the track 185 to 190 miles an hour. Your eyes have to look where the car needs to go.

---

114 Coleman, Ken. "#96: Tom Ziglar--The Keys to Top Performance". Podcast. The Entreleadership Podcast, 2015.

115 Ibid.

At that speed, if you look at the wall, you hit the wall." Tom was amazed at the illustration and tells the story to reinforce the importance of putting into your mind what you hope to get out.

Tom shared one last story to explain the impact of having a positive attitude. Tom mentioned that every time he gets on an airplane, he gives a gift to every member of the flight crew. The gift is a pocket-size book of quotes that costs less than one dollar, with a Starbucks gift card inside of it.

Tom said that every time he gets on a plane, he asks the first flight attendant he sees if they can help him with his goal. After they ask him what his goal is, he'll say how he is "trying to have the best travel year ever." He then goes on to explain that if the flight attendants are happy then he will most likely be happy. At the conclusion of that dialogue, Tom hands them the book with the Starbucks gift card in it and expresses his appreciation for the work that they do despite the lack of recognition they receive. Tom then does the same thing for each flight attendant on the plane and asks one of them to deliver two gifts to the pilots as well.

As a result of this appreciation, Tom said that the atmosphere typically changes instantly. He mentioned receiving hand-written notes, seat upgrades, extra snacks and beverages, and overall better customer service. Although Tom does not provide the gifts and words of appreciation to receive benefits in return, it almost always happens. Tom closed out his interview by saying, "If we're going to work on our attitude, effort, and skill, why not take it a step further into the realm of significance?" Tom suggests that we all "try to impact somebody else's attitude by showing gratitude for them and appreciation."[116]

Now that we understand the impact that attitude, effort, and skill can have on performance, let's discuss how to handle your high performers.

HIGH-POTENTIAL EMPLOYEES

A good talent management program will help identify high-potential employees. I like to define high-potential employees as those who have the competence and confidence to take on more responsibility in the future. High-potential employees typically are aspirational in nature. They typically possess a level of ambition. Any talent management program should enhance an employee's ability to be successful.

A key to optimizing talent management is making employee development part of your organizational culture. When growth and development are at your core, it becomes much easier to focus on leadership skills and behaviors that contribute to superior performance. Articulating key competencies will allow you to clarify expectations with your team. You always want your team to know what success looks like.

The integration of behavior, core values, vision, and mission is a tough thing to accomplish with talent management. However, the alignment of organizational purpose and employee performance can lead to a competitive advantage

---

116 Ibid.

in your industry. Performance reviews and bonuses should reinforce the behavior you want to see replicated. Ideally, the competencies you use to evaluate your employees align with each of your core values. Try creating an employee growth plan for each team member.

This growth plan will align both parties to what success looks like short and long term. This will also show your employees that you are interested in their ideal career path or progression. I recommend exposing employees to a variety of experiences to prepare them for more responsibility. That is why expatriate programs, rotational programs, and special projects often lead to promotions within organizations. According to the 70-20-10 Model for Learning and Development, education, exposure, and experience are all important for employee development.[117] Below is how the three rank, in order of importance:

1. Education (important)—10 percent
2. Exposure (more important)—20 percent
3. Experience (most important)—70 percent

Leaders need to be transparent with new hires and leaders must also understand that they are responsible for making sure their employees get trained. Hiring is a very important task that should not be taken lightly, and managers should work very hard to build a cohesive team. Ultimately, you must hire the right person for the job and the company as close to 100 percent of the time as possible. You are much

---

117 "The 70-20-10 Model for Learning and Development," Training Industry, January 28, 2014.

more likely to motivate and retain someone if they align with the mission, vision, and values of your organization. Ensuring new hires are a cultural fit will help the training, delegating, supervising, and accountability stages of the Circle of Leadership.

***

TEACH, COACH, TRAIN

Let's take a moment to debrief what we have learned so far in this chapter. We discussed the theory of perfect practice making perfect when it comes to training. An effective talent management initiative should leverage culture to achieve results. Talent development is at its peak when there's alignment between talent development strategy and overall business goals including mission, vision, and values. Focus on purpose, people, and processes to drive results, and hold leaders accountable by measuring KPIs such as productivity, engagement, and retention.

CONTEXT

We've discussed how culture influences behavior and how behavior drives results. An inspiring purpose will help attract diverse top talent. Once you acquire top talent, you must work hard to train and retain those individuals. In the next chapter, we will discuss the art of delegation and how it can maximize performance. We will cover topics such as establishing trust, testing comprehension, and avoiding pitfalls of delegation.

ACTIVITY:

1. Many employees are attracted to an organization because of growth opportunities. Many employees also leave their organizations due to a lack of growth opportunities. What role does employee development and training play on an employee's perception of growth potential?

2. What would you do if you continued to teach, coach, and train a team member, but they were consistently performing below standard? How many times would you attempt to develop them before deciding it is not a good fit?

3. What is your philosophy on an effective training program? Think about a training program you experienced that was good. Now compare that experience with a poor training program. Compare and contrast them both.

Picture This: In order to set your employees up for success and continue to help them grow, you must effectively teach, coach, and train them. Focusing on talent management will help you create an award-winning employee development plan which serves as the beginning of the "Process" stage of The Circle of Leadership framework.

CHAPTER 9:

THE ART OF DELEGATION

"Too many workplaces are driven by cynicism, paranoia, and self-interest. But the best ones foster trust and cooperation because their leaders build what Simon calls a 'Circle of Safety' that separates the security inside the team from the challenges outside."

—SIMON SINEK

***

MICROSOFT

Imagine walking into a meeting located at the headquarters of one of the largest technology companies in the world. Upon entry, you find a group of professionals having one of the most ardent conversations you've ever heard. So much so that you can't help but wonder if they are angry with each other. Based on your observation, would you say that team has a strong culture or weak culture? If your answer is weak, you are incorrect.

This scene is precisely what Dr. Phillip Powell witnessed walking into a meeting at Microsoft in the '90s. Dr. Powell is the Associate Dean of Academic Programs, as well as the Clinical Associate Professor of Business Economics and Public Policy, for the Kelley School of Business in Indianapolis, Indiana. According to Dr. Powell, he walked into the office at Microsoft to help design an online education program for them and remembered seeing people "going at each other's throat with intense arguments." In fact, "hyper-competitive" was how Dr. Powell described the scene. As he walked out of Microsoft, he couldn't help but reflect on how dynamic the culture was and how much trust must have been established within the team to be able to engage in such fierce dialogue.

Eliminating ego is crucial for establishing trust and minimizing dysfunction within any organization and that is precisely what Microsoft was able to do. Ultimately, Dr. Powell believes that "the most toxic thing in business is ego" and "Confidence with ego is arrogance." He also shared that "Ego without confidence is insecurity."

Insecure leaders are unlikely to get the most out of their teams, so this should be avoided at all costs. Dr. Powell shared, "Insecure people put themselves first" which is the opposite of what highly effective leaders do. People strive to feel safe with their leader and Dr. Powell believes "We don't feel safe with insecure leaders." Instead, leaders must exude confidence without ego in order to build trust with their team. As I continued to research the roles trust and safety played in high-performing organizations, I was fascinated with what I discovered.

LEADERS EAT LAST

Episode seventy-five of *The Entreleadership Podcast* featured best-selling author Simon Sinek. Sinek is the creator of the "Start With Why" TED Talk in 2009, which became the third most-watched video on TED.com, with over 40 million views and subtitled in forty-seven languages.[118] Sinek took the opportunity to explain the inspiration behind his book *Why Leaders Eat Last*. The book explores the key to establishing trust in a team setting and why that is important.

After spending time with leaders in the military, Sinek discovered the significant levels of trust that existed between leaders and their teams. Sinek became deeply fascinated with the amount of cooperation in this setting, which triggered him to explore why this same level of trust was not commonplace in traditional business settings. At the root of Sinek's exploration of trust within teams was leadership. The kind of leadership where the well-being of people is the focus, even beyond the individual desires of the leader. This type of servant-leadership is the foundation of building trust within a team and the leader must take responsibility for creating that atmosphere.

---

118 Simon Sinek, "Leaders Eat Last," Accessed May 25, 2020.

After asking Lieutenant General George Flynn what makes the US Marines so great, Sinek recalled Flynn explaining how the Marine Corps views leadership as more about responsibility than rank. This philosophy is evident if you simply look at how marines line up when it is time to eat. According to Sinek, "the most junior person eats first, and the most senior person eats last."[119] The order of rank determines how the team eats, even though it's not necessarily a written rule. This culture of "leaders eating last" and serving your team first is true servant-leadership at its core. Leadership is about service and responsibility; however, in the business world, leaders often abuse their titles and put their interests first. In high-performing organizations such as the military, the success of the organization is valued above the accomplishments of the individual.

When describing the differences in leadership culture between high-performing and lower-performing organizations, Sinek

---

119 Coleman, Ken. "#75: Simon Sinek—Why Leaders Eat Last". Podcast. The Entreleadership Podcast, 2015.

explains how truth and honesty are essential. The result of a lack of trust in a military environment can lead to death. Sinek believes that is a big reason why we see such high levels of performance produced in these environments. If leaders replicated the importance of truth and honesty in business settings like it's done in the military, organizations would experience much better performance. A long-term, sustainable approach to leadership will beat a short-sighted approach in the long run.

CIRCLE OF SAFETY

Safety is another key ingredient Sinek introduces when it comes to high-performing teams. Sinek states, "When I talk about feeling safe at work, I don't mean the absence of danger."[120] He goes on to reference that danger exists every day in a military environment, however, the danger is external rather than internal. If organizations could replicate this environment and eliminate the fear of each other—that is, fear rooted internally—they could reach higher levels of production.

External threats are typically less likely to be controlled by senior leadership than internal threats. According to Sinek, the question that leaders need to ask is whether their teams feel the need to protect themselves from each other or external factors. Sinek goes on to state, "The more we protect ourselves from each other, the more we weaken the organization as a whole."[121]

---

120 Ibid.
121 Ibid.

I personally have had friends in my network who have shared stories with me about them feeling the need to protect themselves at work. Often this was accomplished by keeping track of their contributions to be able to prove to their leader if needed that they were valuable to the organization. This type of behavior is what Sinek encourages leaders to eliminate from their organizations. By fostering an environment of internal fear, the results are low morale and even lower productivity.

To further drive home his point, Sinek shared a story about a time when he was waiting to board a plane. While waiting to get on his flight, Sinek recalled seeing a guy attempting to board the plane before his group was called to board. Appalled at how poorly the gate agents treated the man, Sinek asked the agents why they treated him poorly for simply trying to board the plane early. The gate agent responded by saying, "If I don't follow the rules, I could get in trouble or lose my job."[122] Clearly revealing fear of internal circumstances (losing her job) over external circumstances (customer service), this agent is the perfect example of what leaders should try to avoid.

If you compare this story with most experiences at Southwest Airlines, they are two very different experiences. Southwest does not have access to superior talent, but they make a point to hire great people and train them effectively. The leadership at Southwest realizes the importance of their team not fearing leadership. Leaders instill in their teams the importance

---

122 Ibid.

of focusing on the customer above all else. The end result of this culture is excellent customer service.

"The problem is that most of our CEOs of at least public corporations are incentivized by short-term gains, and most of them don't last very long," according to Sinek.[123]

Sinek referenced former General Electric CEO Jack Welch as an example. Although Welch was considered a great leader in the '80s and '90s, Sinek revealed that GE "needed a $300 billion bailout" from the government after 2008.[124] If such a large bailout was necessary, how strong of a foundation did the organization truly have?

That is the question that Sinek presents as he makes his short- vs. long-term approach argument. Sinek goes on to compare GE to Costco, a company that has long been considered an employee- and customer-focused company. Costco has not seen sharp increases in stock price like GE, however, since Costco went public in 1985, you've seen "a slow, steady, very stable growth" according to Sinek.[125] Sinek goes on to state that the same dollar invested in Costco and GE when Costco first went public would have led to similar increases in money without the variability that has taken place with GE. In the long term, slow and steady wins the race—especially when investing in the right things, like people.

---

123 Ibid.
124 Ibid.
125 Ibid.

Before you can effectively delegate anything, you must establish a level of trust. The safety that trust provides will allow you as a leader to empower your team. Clearly articulated expectations and adequate training are both requirements for successful delegation. Let's dive into the art of delegation.

WHAT IS DELEGATION?

Delegation is dividing and conquering. Delegation is spreading the workload for the sake of teamwork, work/life balance, and overall performance.

> ## Delegation is empowering others with the authority to make decisions.

Although tasks are often delegated, providing the authority to make decisions regarding those tasks is what is most important. What better way to show your team how much you trust them than by delegating important tasks to them?

Effectively delegating is a productivity multiplier.

You can cover more ground faster by delegating properly. Unfortunately, many leaders struggle with delegation, and therefore are unable to tap into the power that comes with that function of leadership.

I want to specify that you should not blindly trust someone. You have to inspect something you expect—meaning you can trust an employee but still verify they are performing the task correctly. Supervising an employee and providing feedback does not mean you do not trust them. You are simply doing your job as a leader to test comprehension. Below are three steps that will help you effectively delegate and develop trust:

1. Articulate the Why
   - When your team is aware of the larger purpose behind a task, they are much more likely to make good decisions. Knowing the motivation behind work helps team members to have a long-term perspective even if the task is short term in nature. Articulating the "why" behind a delegated task also reinforces organizational culture.
2. Clarify Expectations
   — Before you delegate a task you not only have to articulate the "why," you must clarify what success looks like. By painting a picture for your team to follow, you are clarifying expectations, which will make it easier for you to provide feedback. When expectations are

not clarified and agreed on, you as the leader are just as much at fault if the task does not get completed appropriately.

3. Follow Through and Feedback

— Once you are on the same page with your team, you must put yourself in a position to supervise their performance. By supervising the performance of your team, you will be able to observe behaviors that you can help them improve. Hopefully, the result of your supervision will lead to you giving your team praise and appreciation for a job well done! Feedback is a gift so be happy to provide it to your team.

I have seen the benefits of communication leading to better teamwork. Dating back to my time at Indiana University, I was the former President of The Gamma Eta Chapter of Alpha Phi Alpha Fraternity Inc. As a leader amongst leaders, it was my first experience being challenged as a leader. One of the key ways I was able to get buy-in from the members in my fraternity was by opening the lines of communication and creating an environment where we could be vulnerable—starting with me. Vulnerability in an organizational setting helps to create transparency and empathy, which are important when it comes to relationship-building.

At the conclusion of my tenure as president, I was told by my District Director that I was the best chapter president he had seen in the state of Indiana. I truly believe that the members of the organization and the culture that the leadership team created were major reasons why our chapter was so successful.

MAXIMIZING YOUR RESOURCES

In order to maximize your human capital, you have to provide your people with the tools and resources to win. Your job as the coach is to put the ball in the hands of your playmakers. Acknowledging that someone on your team might be better at a particular task than you is okay. One of the wonderful things about teamwork is recognizing where one person lacks and another person is proficient.

You should work to understand the strengths and weaknesses of your team. If you know what your employees are good at, you can better delegate tasks to them. The alignment of delegated tasks, skill, and will can increase the chances of successful performance from your team.

Another strategy that can lead to effective delegation is modeling the behavior for your team. By showing your subordinates that you are willing to do any task that you delegate to them, you increase credibility and trustworthiness. Be cautious of having a mentality of being too good to do any particular task. Great leaders lead the way by casting vision and leading the group verbally and by their actions.

Growing your business is largely determined by the effectiveness of your leadership and your people. As a leader, you must create a culture where effective delegation is the norm. It takes more than good talent to be good at delegation. Patience, competence, emotional intelligence, and training will help you maximize your resources.

Now that we have covered the importance of delegation and how trust and training should be at the foundation of that leadership function, let's cover some reasons why delegation often fails.

I DON'T TRUST YOU

I once had a store manager named Judy. She was very hard-working, but she struggled with delegation. After consistently working eighty-plus hours a week and having a heart attack (literally), she finally came to her senses about overworking herself. Judy's inability and unwillingness to delegate was stifling her store's potential and her personal health.

Judy's store was very busy and experienced a 25 percent sales growth over the previous year. Judy's store was also about to undergo a remodel, which historically led to a 15–20 percent lift on sales. Realizing what was soon to come for Judy and her team, I began trying to change her perspective on delegation so she could work fewer hours and improve her health and work/life balance.

"If you're working these many hours now, how many more hours will you work per week when your sales and customer count doubles?" I stated to Judy. By challenging Judy to start small and slowly give up responsibility, she started seeing small wins. Certain tasks that she had become accustomed to completing were suddenly given to her highly competent and now fully trained team to execute. Luckily, Judy finally saw the big picture and began to change her ways.

Judy's dilemma is one that countless leaders experience every day. Below are some of the most common reasons I've found that leaders do not delegate:

- Leaders think they can do the job better or quicker than anyone else
- Leaders enjoy the sense of accomplishing a task and crossing it off their to-do list
- Leaders like to feel valued and important
- Leaders do not trust their employees
- Leaders are afraid of an employee becoming a threat to their job security

ROOT CAUSE

Shane Fimbel is the Chief Executive Officer of a technology company based out of South Bend, Indiana called Trek10, Inc. Shane graduated from Wabash College in 2002 and later completed his PhD in Neuroscience from The University of Notre Dame. As an entrepreneur and former Adjunct Professor at Purdue University-Krannert School of Management, Shane has a unique approach to leadership.

When I spoke to Shane about his perspective on delegation, I asked him why some leaders struggle with that function of business. According to Shane, "People who have a failure to delegate is because they think they can do it faster and better than someone else." In other words, the root of poor delegation often stems from a lack of trust.

Although the reason why a leader fails to effectively delegate varies, the consequences of not delegating are almost universal. In Judy's case, she did not trust her employees and therefore felt like her doing the job was the only way to ensure it got done and got done correctly.

Often when leaders shy away from providing constructive criticism, it can impact delegation. The true issue Judy was dealing with was a lack of training and accountability. She had assisted in the hiring process and selected the right candidates and thought she trained them appropriately, but she never addressed poor performance head-on by holding herself and her team accountable. Instead, she refrained from delegating to them, which stifled their growth.

Luckily, I was able to assist Judy with improving her delegation skills. However, I was not always able to effectively delegate. I learned the skill the hard way years ago.

DELEGATING DONE WRONG

Six months into my first major entrepreneurial endeavor, I found myself breaking the cardinal sin of delegation. As the co-founder of a branding and consulting firm called Handy-Brand, I had a business partner I needed to trust. Unfortunately, I only trusted him to a certain extent, which interfered with our business operationally. Although extremely talented, my co-founder was terrible at meeting deadlines and returning phone calls and emails in a timely fashion. His continued issues with communication and punctuality led to me micromanaging tasks I would delegate to him.

In fact, sometimes I would even refrain from delegating tasks to him at all to avoid friction. Not delegating also seemed like the better option because I felt I could complete the task more efficiently than my partner. This behavior was obviously not conducive to a good business and a good partnership. I found myself doing the majority of the work and not holding him accountable for his shortcomings. Ultimately, we closed the firm down due to a lack of trust and communication.

Delegation does not mean that you hand off tasks and responsibilities to anyone. Delegation is a process that your team must show they are capable of handling. Delegation can be time-consuming but fulfilling when done right. Trust, integrity, competence, and confidence are all ingredients for delegation done right.

Ultimately, a culture of effective delegation is one where your team can begin to anticipate your needs and execute within their realm of responsibility and authority.

Be cautious to not devalue the task you're delegating, as this will lower the likelihood of optimal execution. As we have covered earlier in this book, training is also key. By clarifying expectations, articulating the "why" behind the delegated responsibility, and avoiding the trap of micromanaging the task(s) you've delegated, you will be in prime position to hold your team accountable.

Excellent cultures have tremendous levels of trust and trust is at the core of delegation. The result of Judy not trusting in her team was devastating. It not only interfered with her ability to delegate, but it also interfered with her being able to build a culture of trust in her store. Fortunately for her, she was able to turn things around. If she can do that, so can you.

MYCHAEL SPENCER

As a former Teach for America leader and principal in Indiana, Mychael Spencer is well aware of the components of delegation and accountability. Spencer got his bachelor's degree from Indiana University and his master's degree from Columbia University. Currently, Spencer is the Managing Director of Business Operations for KIPP Indy charter school network. Spencer believes that top-down leadership is outdated and is typically not good especially for millennials and future generations. As the approach of "you do this because I said so" continues to miss the mark, leaders will have to continue to be collaborative and empowering to get the most out of their people when delegating. Spencer believes that "good leadership is where you use skills, talents, and resources to influence others."

When describing an ideal culture, Spencer said, "Good culture is where you can bring your whole self to the workplace." When you allow your team to fail safely, you create a culture of calculated risk-taking, which will help breed innovation and creativity. When asked about delegation and accountability, Spencer shared that the "only thing to hold someone accountable for is learning from mistakes." Leaders must work to create environments where failure is encouraged and you "can bring your whole self to the workplace," according to Spencer. However, this is not feasible without a culture of trust.

Spencer believes if leaders put the right emphasis on hiring the right people and training appropriately, that delegation and accountability should be simple. "I don't want you to give me who you want to be, I want you to be who you are," stated Spencer when describing his mentality toward creating a safe space for applicants and team members. When creating and leveraging culture, it is vital to create a safe and open environment so that you can have an engaged and productive workforce. According to Spencer, "Accountability without support is punitive and toxic."

As a leader, be sure to hold your team accountable by being clear, consistent, and fair. Supervision is one of the first steps when it comes to accountability. You've got to show your team you are watching their work and willing to provide feedback. We will outline the keys to creating a culture of accountability in the next chapter of this book.

***

CONTEXT

Let's take a moment to debrief what we have learned so far. The Circle of Leadership was created on the belief of the power of culture in driving results. Your "why," or in other words, organizational purpose, is important to clarify before hiring people. Selecting great candidates does not matter if you cannot retain them.

Trust is at the center of delegation. Without it, you are less likely to get the full potential out of your team. Delegation is empowering others with the authority to make decisions. Maximizing resources is a skill that all leaders should try to possess because it helps improve efficiency while simultaneously empowering your team. In order to effectively delegate, you must articulate the "why" behind the task, clarify expectations, and hold team members accountable by providing timely feedback.

ACTIVITY:
1. Why do you think leaders struggle with delegation? How would you coach a leader who struggles with delegation?
2. What do you believe is the most valuable reward of delegation? Have you experienced this benefit or witnessed it? If so, describe how it made you or another person feel.
3. What are some of the first types of decisions you should be delegated as a leader? What things should not be delegated?

Picture This: Successful leaders learn to master the art of delegation. This crucial step requires building trust and is critical to achieving success within the "Process" stage of The Circle of Leadership framework.

CHAPTER 10:

ACCOUNTABILITY (EXTREME OWNERSHIP)

"We have to be able to take feedback—regardless of how it's delivered—and apply it productively."

—BRENÉ BROWN

***

EXTREME OWNERSHIP

The sound of machine guns, bombs going off, and other heavy artillery is common when you're a US Navy SEAL in the heat of battle. Countless hours of training and preparation are a must in order for this elite group of heroes to perform at the highest level. As you can imagine, exceptional leadership can be the difference between life or death when strategizing to defeat the enemy. Several leadership characteristics are vital for success, but one characteristic among all others reign supreme: extreme ownership.

Best-selling authors and US Navy SEALs Jocko Willink and Leif Babin wrote a book titled *Extreme Ownership*. The book uncovers leadership principles for winning both on the battlefield and in the boardroom. Willink and Babin share in their book the single most important leadership trait comes down to leaders taking accountability for everything that happens within their realm of responsibility. "Extreme ownership" is the phrase the authors use to describe this mentality. They've seen firsthand that it serves as the key to victory—both in business and war.

In *Extreme Ownership*, the authors make it clear that although the stakes may be higher in a military setting, it is a myth that people follow leadership blindly. The authors make the case that military personnel are purpose-driven individuals who are the ultimate team players. The trust established in military settings is crucial for their overall success—similar to business settings. According to the authors, "Combat leadership requires getting a diverse team of people in various groups to execute highly complex missions in order to achieve strategic goals—something that directly correlates with any company or organization."[126]

Effective leaders know how to win regardless of the industry. The most effective leaders understand the importance of teamwork and pushing your team to levels they would not be able to reach alone. Leaders cast vision and set expectations for their team to follow.

---

126 Willink Jocko and Leif Babin, *Extreme Ownership: How US Navy SEALs Lead and Win*, Sydney, N.S.W.: Macmillan, 2018.

According to *Extreme Ownership*, Babin and Willink share that "when it comes to standards, as a leader, it's not what you preach, it's what you tolerate. When setting expectations, no matter what has been said or written, if substandard performance is accepted and no one is held accountable—if there are no consequences—that poor performance becomes the new standard. Therefore, leaders must enforce standards. Consequences for failing need not be immediately severe, but leaders must ensure that tasks are repeated until the higher expected standard is achieved."[127]

Extreme ownership is synonymous with extreme accountability. The only distinction is that leaders must strive to first hold themselves accountable before holding anyone else accountable. Let's take a deeper look at what accountability looks like.

_____

127 Ibid.

ACCOUNTABILITY IN ACTION

I once had a tenured manager who had been working for the company longer than I had been alive. In fact, her first district manager was the CEO of the company at the time I was her leader. With that being said, she had cemented her place in the organization, even though her performance and overall store conditions were lackluster.

It did not take me long to realize that she was struggling. Everything at her store, from retention, to significant wasted product, to sales, to customer service was far below her peers, who had much less experience than her. What really made the situation challenging was that she was one of the nicest people I have ever met. Her energy was infectious, and her positive spirit radiated to employees and customers. You would think with a personality like that, she would have been able to obtain better results. However, that was not the case.

After months of working with her and providing resources and training, it became evident that she was no longer capable of doing the job well. Ultimately, she was not the leader we needed to train the staff and hold the team accountable. She avoided having tough conversations with her team in an effort to not cause tension in her store. She also did not adequately train her team and tried to do all the work herself. Her poor leadership led to her termination after months of trying to coach her.

I was expecting some serious backlash from her team during my first visit to her store after she was fired. I was shocked to find out that her team was happy she was let go. I heard from several employees that although she was very nice, she did not develop the team or hold anyone accountable, which upset a lot of people. That day I realized not only is there such a thing as good turnover but also not making tough decisions to let people go can lead to turnover with your good performers.

DOES GOOD TURNOVER EXIST?

The answer is yes. Good turnover does exist. And if you don't have any, you may have an accountability problem. Recognizing that you do not want to retain every single employee that you have is important. You should strive to retain all of the good employees you have and get rid of the poor-performing employees.

Retaining poor performers can have a negative impact on employee morale, customer service, and overall business performance. People do not want to work with incompetent, poor-performing people. Not getting rid of bad employees can also cause your good employees to leave. You want to coach and develop your poor performers to help them improve, but if that method continues to be unsuccessful, you must make the tough decision to let them go.

Think about it like this. Poor-performing team members have essentially terminated themselves by knowing the standard and consistently not meeting it.

PROMOTING PEOPLE TO CUSTOMER

If you've read through the previous chapters in this book, you understand the importance of putting "who" before "what" and taking time to get the right person in the right seat on the bus. Now it's time to focus on the process of letting someone go. One of my former employees once told me that the process of letting someone go was simply "promoting them to customer." Although I was able to find humor in that statement, there are some good takeaways from that comment.

Regardless of the offense, you should treat your team members with respect. You should not shy away from addressing problems you have with your team. However, there are ways you can put your foot down without stomping it. Be tough on the behavior but easy on the person.

One question to ask yourself after delivering some tough feedback or even terminating someone is "Will this person still want to be a customer for us?" Even though it may be unlikely for the answer to be yes, you should strive for it to be. If you are able to accomplish that, you have most likely been fair and respectful throughout the disciplinary process. In order to position yourself for fair and consistent performance management, I recommend the following steps:

THREE STRIKES AND YOU'RE OUT

1. Verbal warning

A verbal warning should be just that—a private, verbal coaching conversation. This conversation should include you reiterating the expectation, identifying how their performance/behavior is not meeting that expectation, and providing resources and recommendations for improvement. It is important to ask if they have any questions or need any clarification.

You also want to make sure they understand what failure to meet expectations will lead to, which is a written warning. Clarifying the deadline for performance or behavior to improve is important. Although this performance management step is called a "verbal warning," I highly recommend documenting the details of the behavior, as well as the details of the conversation. This will help you if you have to take further disciplinary action down the road.

2. Written Warning

The second step to the performance management process is a written warning. This process should take place after a team member has been administered a verbal warning and given the necessary tools and coaching for improvement but are still not meeting expectations. This step should include a review of the prior verbal warning conversation as well as a discussion on how the team member is still not meeting expectations.

This step is crucial as it serves as their second strike. Just like baseball, three strikes and you're out! You want to get commitment from the team member on their action plan for improvement. You also want to verify that their poor performance is not a result of poor leadership or lack of training. Once you can get the team member to admit there is nothing else you can provide to help them succeed, you must clearly articulate what continued failure will lead to.

3. Final Warning

The final step prior to termination is the final warning. As the title states, it's a team member's last chance for improvement. This step should review previous steps in the performance management process. Let them know that any further infractions within the realm of performance/behavioral issues previously addressed will result in termination.

If another violation occurs, the employee should not even bother to show up to work, unless it's to pack up their personal belongings. In almost a decade of following these performance management steps, I can tell you that very rarely will a team member remain a long-term employee for you once they've gotten to a final warning. If you follow these three steps, you are much more likely to feel comfortable with the decision to let someone go. The truth of the matter is they let themselves go.

Please note that egregious offenses such as discrimination, harassment, theft, violence, and other detrimental conduct should result in termination much quicker. Most of the time, you'll find that someone who violates serious codes of conduct should be terminated immediately. Remember, your team is watching. Do the right thing and set the tone with your team. It will help reinforce an award-winning culture.

Now that we have covered the performance management process for holding team members accountable, let's review a tool that an expert in the field created to help you execute accountability at a high level.

DARE TO LEAD

In Brené Brown's best-selling book *Dare to Lead*, she talks about a resource called "The Accountability and Success

Checklist."[128] This checklist is a resource that leaders can utilize to clarify expectations and supervise their teams effectively and efficiently. The framework of the checklist consists of (T)-Task, (A)-Accountability, (S)-Success, and (C)-Checklist. Below is an overview of each component:

Task
Task pertains to who owns the task. Task is important to identify so you know who to hold accountable for the results and overall execution of it.

Accountability
Accountability pertains to the person in charge of the task being given proper authority to being held accountable.

Success
Success pertains to whether or not the necessary resources, time, and tools have been provided to ensure success.

Checklist
Checklist pertains to having a systematic process to document and track progress such as this checklist.

By using a resource such as the "Accountability and Success Checklist," Brené believes leaders and organizations will be much more equipped to foster environments with high levels of accountability. Articulate to your team what success looks like in excruciating detail in order to give your team the highest probability of success. According to Brené, "This

---

128 Brené Brown, *Dare to Lead: Brave Work, Tough Conversations, Whole Hearts*, Random House Large Print Publishing, 2019.

is a guideline for readiness."[129] She then goes on to provide a thought process that leaders should go through to ensure they are adequately prepared to deliver feedback to a team member.

Here are some pieces of advice for having tough conversations and providing productive feedback:[130]

1. Show that you are on their side and want them to succeed. This can only be accomplished through genuine levels of empathy and transparency.
2. Practice active listening while having the accountability discussion. You should be facilitating rather than preaching during your conversation.
3. Don't hesitate to give yourself more time prior to making a decision. Sometimes you will be thrown a curveball during your discussion and you do not want to make a bad decision due to not giving yourself ample time to think it through.
4. Always attempt to highlight positive performance and behavior that you would like to see continued.
5. Take extreme ownership over things that fall within your realm of responsibility as their leader. Since your team is your responsibility, chances are you have played a part in their failure in one way, shape, or form.
6. Try to leave the conversation inspiring the team member to improve performance. Find ways to motivate them to accomplish their personal and professional goals especially ones that mutually benefit the company.

---

129 Ibid.
130 Ibid.

Although being held accountable isn't always fun, it's always necessary. The best way to learn to value feedback is to realize that it will only make you better. Learn to view feedback and accountability as a gift.

FEEDBACK IS A GIFT

Leaders must be able to provide feedback and address performance and behavior issues in a timely fashion. Leveraging systems and processes can help tremendously with holding team members accountable. Something as simple as an organizational system can help leaders better execute and prioritize following up with their team.

In order to solve problems, you must be in a position to truly understand the problem. In the leadership world, this is called supervising. As a leader, you must supervise anything that you delegate. This simple action plays a significant role in positioning yourself to give effective feedback.

Feedback is a gift and should be happily given and received. However, this is usually not the case due to lack of trust, lack of timely or consistent feedback, poor delivery of feedback, and more. When executed properly, you will be able to supervise your team, provide timely feedback and coaching, and ultimately hold your team accountable.

***

ACCOUNTABILITY IN A NUTSHELL

In closing, fostering an environment of extreme ownership is critical for a culture of accountability. Although we want to minimize turnover in general, there is such a thing as good turnover. Leaders must be fair, consistent, and intentional with personnel issues to ensure they are making appropriate decisions. Supervision and feedback are instrumental in holding your team accountable. If you can get your people to treat feedback as a gift, you are well on your way to creating an award-winning organizational culture rooted in accountability and extreme ownership.

CONTEXT

The Circle of Leadership is not complete without account-ability. In order to foster a culture of extreme ownership, you must first identify your purpose and then hire "A" players to help push that mission forward. After you train your team and test their comprehension through delegation, you must supervise your team to maximize performance. Proper supervision and coaching will lead to a culture of productive feedback, extreme ownership, and accountability.

Accountability shows your team that you are watching. It shows that you care. It shows you care so much about them being successful that you are willing to let them go if they can no longer be successful within your organization. Brené Brown states in *Dare to Lead* that "we have to be able to take feedback—regardless of how it's delivered—and apply it pro-ductively. We have to do this for a simple reason: Mastery requires feedback. I don't care what we're trying to mas-ter—and whether we're trying to develop greatness or pro-ficiency—it always requires feedback."[131]

ACTIVITY:

1. How would you describe accountability?
2. What obstacles do you think typically get in the way of leaders holding their teams accountable?
3. What is the most challenging part of holding someone accountable for their actions, behavior, and performance?

---

131 Ibid.

Picture This: As the last leg in the "Process" stage of The Circle of Leadership, a culture of accountability validates all the previous components of the framework. Holding yourself and others accountable is a major step in creating an environment of extreme ownership.

CONCLUSION: FULL CIRCLE

"A great company is marked by a culture of discipline, self-disciplined people who engage in disciplined thought and take disciplined action."

— JIM COLLINS

***

RETURN ON CULTURE (ROC)

Imagine you're the CEO of a large organization and you find yourself struggling to retain your top performers. You realize that your competitors are plucking your "A" players from your roster. This leaves you and your senior leadership team scratching your heads and wondering why. Then suddenly, an idea gets thrown on the table regarding how to solve the problem: spend several thousand—if not millions—of dollars to renovate the headquarters. What would you say? What would you think? This unique suggestion turned reality is one of the pivotal steps that changed the culture at Land O'Lakes.

Founded in 1921, Land O'Lakes is "a market-and customer-driven cooperative committed to optimizing the value of our members' dairy, crop and livestock production."[132] According to Michael Brown, Director of Strategic Sourcing at Land O'Lakes, roughly four or five years ago, Land O'Lakes was losing talent to their competitors, and they wanted to figure out why. So, the company set out to determine why they were not getting top talent and retaining that talent. At the conclusion of their quest for reflection and discovery, the organization determined that their problems began at the cubicles they worked in at the corporate headquarters (HQ).

After continuously losing talent to competitors, they soon realized that their HQ was much different than competitors. Michael described their old HQ as something you would see in the '90s. Enclosed working stations that stifled

---

132 Land O'Lakes, Accessed May 25, 2020.

communication and outdated decor and equipment were commonplace at the HQ. It became clear that their competitors had much more modern HQs than them. Ultimately, they realized that it was a cultural thing that was causing people to go to competitors.

Even without overly specific details on how a new HQ would impact the bottom line, the company knew it was still the right decision to make. The building would play a large role in creating the collaborative and modern culture they were trying to create. However, there were opposing views on the justification of the spend on a new building.

Eventually, the leaders of the organization made the investment with the hopes of retaining top talent and positively impacting culture. The organizational culture was improved through several initiatives, but the largest change stemmed from creating a more open work environment with no assigned seating in the new building. The building was eventually opened, and it did exactly what it was supposed to do. It shifted the culture and created a more open and collaborative work environment which they found appealed more to the people they were trying to recruit. The end result was improved recruiting and retention efforts.

Michael articulated that the company had a clear why for their actions. "What's the reason you're doing what you're doing?" is a question Michael believes all leaders should regularly ask themselves and others. Sure, Land O'Lakes spent time looking at certain indicators about the endeavor they were considering, but ultimately, they prioritized their people over profits knowing that attracting and retaining the right people would make the investment worth it. Land O'Lakes was able to determine that the return on culture was well worth it.

My conversation with Michael helped reinforce a few thoughts:

1. Sometimes leaders have to trust their gut and make decisions they know will positively impact people and culture instead of overly focusing on the return on investment (ROI) from a numerical standpoint.
2. Organizational culture absolutely influences employee retention.

***

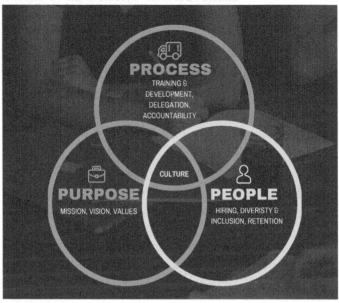

CULTIVATING CULTURE

When implementing the Circle of Leadership framework used in this book, it is important to remember that culture is the unwritten, yet commonly shared set of beliefs that guide behavior. As we learned from the "$6,000 Egg" story, it is the responsibility of senior leadership to influence and promote a healthy organizational culture, which can lead to superior performance compared to firms with weaker cultures. According to Gallup, "Highly engaged workplaces see a 10 percent increase in customer ratings and a 20 percent increase in sales."[133] Your customers not only expect great customer service, they deserve it.

---

133 Jim Harter and Annamarie Mann. "The Right Culture: Not Just About Employee Satisfaction," Gallup, May 5, 2020.

LEVERAGING CULTURE (80/20 RULE)

If your organization's culture is not where it should be, that is okay. Just like we saw with Stefan Larsson and Old Navy, it is never too late to change culture, but you must be patient yet intentional in order to effectively change it. Take a proactive step toward changing your organization's culture by allocating a portion of your workweek to work on intangibles that will move the culture forward.

> I believe that spending roughly 20 percent of your time on reinforcing positive behaviors can lead to 80 percent of the performance of a company.

If this principle can work for companies like Google and Intuit, it can certainly add value to your organization. Be sure to ask yourself why as much as possible to ensure you are working toward the right goals.

FINDING PURPOSE (MISSION, VISION, VALUES)

In order to create an award-winning culture, you must have a solid foundation. Finding your purpose similar to John O'Leary's igniting fire story can galvanize a team. Inspiring visions such as Dr. Martin Luther King Jr.'s "I Have A Dream" speech can bring people from all different walks of life together. Preserving the core while stimulating progress is a message from Jim Collins that helps reinforce core values.

A compelling and easy to remember **mission, vision,** and set of **core values** help articulate the "why" behind your organization. Clearly defining your "why" can engage your workforce and aid in the decision-making process. Take some time to reflect on the impact of an effective culture and an inspiring purpose. In order to turn your mission into reality, you must continuously articulate the mission to create awareness and understanding in an effort to gain commitment and action.

HIRING

Repetition is key for reinforcing anything with your team. Consistency in your messaging will further ingrain culture into existing team members while creating a foundation for new hires. When it comes to building your team, your people will be your greatest assets so you must be intentional and selective with who you hire. This was extremely important at Disney as we learned from long-time executive Lee Cockerell. We also saw the importance of people through key takeaways from *Good to Great* by Jim Collins.

In addition to being patient throughout the **hiring** process, it's crucial to be consistent and informative. The candidates you interview want to make sure your organization is a good fit for them just like you are evaluating them. Approaching hiring like marriage rather than dating will help set the stage for really getting to know applicants.

Another key ingredient to evaluate is **Emotional Intelligence (EQ).** EQ has been proven to be a common denominator in effective leaders. Try to gauge potential leaders on their emotional intelligence ability during the interview process. Intentionality will help you select the right person for the right job. Remember to get rid of people on your team who are a cancer to the organization. Good performers will eventually leave your company if you do not get rid of the dead weight. It is your responsibility as a leader to help your team grow, even if that means pruning your team to get rid of unproductive team members who are not carrying their weight.

DIVERSITY AND INCLUSION

When hiring, be mindful of the value that comes with having a diverse and inclusive team. Author Kate Johnson showed us how to harness our differences and use them as a differentiator. Cultures that promote **diversity and inclusion** have proven to lead to higher levels of performance. To obtain a competitive advantage through your people, it is important to seek diversity of thought when hiring. By following my diversity and inclusion road map, you will be able to create an initiative that aligns with your overall company strategy. Remember to think through unconscious bias and how that influences behavior. By understanding the barriers of a culture centered around diversity and inclusion, you will be better positioned to overcome those barriers.

THE ART OF RETENTION

Once you acquire top talent, you must work hard to **retain** those individuals. As we learned from the "Bob" story shared by CEO David Novak, it is every leader's duty to appreciate, inspire, and recognize their team. Employee retention can be improved by focusing on the hiring and onboarding process, completing thirty-, sixty-, and ninety-day check-ins, providing adequate training, and offering retention bonuses. Talent development is at its peak when there's alignment between talent development strategy and overall business goals including mission, vision, and values. Focus on purpose, people, and processes to drive results and hold leaders accountable by measuring KPIs such as productivity, engagement, and retention.

TRAINING AND DEVELOPMENT

When it comes to **training and development**, we discovered that perfect practice produces extraordinary results, and one of the ways this can be accomplished is by using the "Performance Formula" brought to us by leadership expert Tom Ziglar. My personal example of my mentor's training methods showed how pivotal training is for long-term success.

THE ART OF DELEGATION

After adequately training your team, it is time to test their comprehension. This can be accomplished most effectively by **delegation**. Trust is at the center of delegation. Without it, you are less likely to get the full potential out of your team. Delegation is empowering others with the authority to make decisions. Maximizing resources is a skill that all leaders should try to possess because it helps improve efficiency and empowers your team. In order to effectively delegate you must articulate the "why" behind the task, clarify expectations, and hold team members accountable by providing timely feedback.

ACCOUNTABILITY (EXTREME OWNERSHIP)

The Circle of Leadership is not complete without **accountability**. Accountability shows your team that you are watching. It shows that you care. It shows that you care so much about them being successful that you are willing to let them go if they can no longer be successful within your organization. Turnover is expensive and should be avoided unless you are dealing with poor performers. Getting rid of people who are not meeting expectations is considered good turnover. There are several ways you can inspire your team by expressing appreciation. The key is to simply take action and do it. Feedback is a gift and should be given out intentionally and willingly. So why focus on culture if you are a leader? Fostering the right organizational culture can lead to a sustainable advantage over your competitors.

If you want to win, focus on leadership and culture. You won't regret it.

***

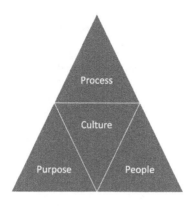

PURPOSE + PEOPLE + PROCESS = CULTURE

There is no finish line for culture. Culture is an ongoing, never-ending race to help team members understand how to behave and make decisions for the betterment of the organization. Leaders must work to minimize negativity in their organizations and that starts with senior leaders. By encouraging team members to be vulnerable, teams are able to create environments where trust is embedded within the culture. I recommend to not underestimate the power of doing work that matters and work that makes you happy. Be authentic because if you are not, your team will notice, and it will undermine your ability to positively influence culture.

Activity:
1. What resonated most with you from The Circle of Leadership? Why?
2. Which portion of The Circle of Leadership would be most challenging to implement? Why? What first step could you take to overcome that?
3. How would you explain The Circle of Leadership to a friend, family member, colleague, etc.?

Picture This: The Circle of Leadership is a framework for implementing excellent leadership and culture. When executed properly, purpose, people, and process can transform your organizational culture, which can improve employee engagement, productivity, and retention.

ACKNOWLEDGMENTS

This book is a culmination of real-life experience, research, primary and secondary interviews, and more. Without the inspiration and knowledge from others, this book would not exist. With that being said, I'd like to acknowledge those who have given this book, and the stories within it, legs strong enough to move forward:

First and foremost, I would like to thank my wife, Tomi Adeniyi for her patience, understanding, critiques, and support as I went through this book-writing process. Without her assistance along the way, this book would not have been able to come to fruition, so thank you.

I would also like to thank my children, Elijah and Shiloh, for serving as inspiration on those late nights and early mornings where I wanted to do everything but write another paragraph. I hope this book inspires you both to accomplish your dreams and share your knowledge with the world.

Thank you to my sisters, Mary and Michelle Adeniyi, for your ongoing support, as well as my parents, Dr. Michael and Grace Adeniyi, for instilling in me the value of education and hard work.

There are also a few sources of inspiration that have been invaluable to me over the years, many of which significantly influenced the content within this book. Below are some of the most prominent resources:

Simon Sinek, Dave Ramsey, Ken Coleman and *The Entreleadership Podcast*, Patrick Lencioni, Lee Cockerell, Deloitte, McKinsey, Jim Collins, Zig Ziglar, Tom Ziglar, David Novak, Daniel Pink, Brené Brown, Jocko Willink, Leif Babin, The Walt Disney Company, Starbucks, Southwest Airlines, Google, IBM, Walmart, Nike, Feeding America, Todd Duncan, Erik Koester, Harvard Business Review, Eli Broad College of Business at Michigan State University, Kelley School of Business at Indiana University Bloomington, Dr. Sanjay Gupta, Judge Andre Gammage, Alex Muñoz, Kate Johnson, Ontay Johnson, Mychael Spencer, David Spencer, Michael Brown, Pastor Kevin Rogers, Trek10, Shane Fimbel, Dr. Phil Powell, and Christy Rutherford.

I'd also like to gratefully acknowledge my beta readers:

Seun Atolagbe, John Barry, Matthew & Victoire Kumalo, Kaley DeVries, Brit'ney Grimes, Arceonul, Moore, Cordaryl Taylor, Frederick Nwanganga, Tammy Reed, Fred Haley Sr., Ashlee Green, Israel Olaore, Angel Shenice, Longino, Eric Goode, Brian Garcia, Valencia Gammage, Devan & Jasmine, Corey Johnson, Marquez Carlisle, AL Hartman, Bernard Mickle, Aleah Jordan, Keon Brown, Olubunmi Amakor, Taren Johnson, Mychael Spencer, Logan Emmitt,

Tiana Iruoje, Aaron Willis, Valentin Emmanuel, Jarrod R. Buchanon, Tomi Adeniyi, Ugo Udeogu, Andrew McKenzie, KJoohnsonBeyond, Michael, Brown, Marc Hardy, Fiyin Fawole, Chelby & Ben Tookey, Danielle Judin, Tyler Rouse, Tewa Oyarinde, Shevora Edy, Berk Koprulu, Mariah Broader, Christian Wellmann, Austin & Katrina Gammage, DeNai Donaville, Luqmann Ruth, Marlon Webb, Olufunso Adeniran, Wole Daramola, Darius & Elilta Sawyers, Omoarukhe Iruoje, Kanteh Kamanda, Krystian Davenport, Lebbaeus Davidson, Blake Batteast, Michael Coleman, Andrew Farinelli, Kell L Golden, Tolulope Apata, Eddie Williams, Joshua Moore, Cameron Harris, Aderonke Olatunji, Landon Davidson, Katie Dincolo, Mary Adeniyi, Ronnie Macheme, Alicia Ivy, Oluwatobi Ajayi, Ifeoluwani Olaore, Brittni King, Sade Ajisegbede, Bosede Apata, Mustapha Baryoh, Tyler Kelley, Sola Lawal, Bunmi Akintomide, D'Juan Wilcher, Temitayo Ade-Oshifogun, Morris Dolley, Danny Fisher, Kaydra Bailey, Lauren McKinney, TJ Lerch, Aaron Laster, Lindsey Reimlinger, Kerry J Phillips, Sequoia Lee, Jennifer Stansberry, Moana Popovich, Meaza Yalew, Mary Oyedijo, Tyiree Phillips, Temitope Ade-Oshifogun, Alan Walker, Aaron Vernon, Nick Vail, Steven Thompson, Matthew Petsche, Forest Bender, William Sanders, Patrick Saint, Brandon Maxwell, William McLaurin, Mike McDonald, Ryan Ligon, Ike Igwe-Onu, Femi Oladunjoye, Walter McDonald, Jeremiah & Selam Reed, Eric Koester, Michelle Adeniyi, Markell & Atinuke Dorsainvil, Michael Burton, Elexis Ackerson, Dr. Olawale & Bosede Ade-Oshifogun, Matthew DeBenedetto, Jonathan Brown, Aaron Barnes, Joey Babka, Seghen Amanios, Larry Davidson, Tre Gammage, and Ross Stuckey.

You all have been instrumental in the writing, revision, and editing process. My book is what it is because of your feedback and support. Thank you for believing in me.

With gratitude,

Andrew Adeniyi

Author | Consultant | Speaker

APPENDIX

———

INTRODUCTION:

Clifton, Jim. "Are You Sure You Have a Great Workplace Culture?" Gallup.com. May 5, 2020. https://www.gallup.com/workplace/236285/sure-great-workplace-culture.aspx.

"Company Culture and Employee Engagement Statistics." CultureIQ, March 19, 2019. https://cultureiq.com/blog/company-culture-employee-engagement-statistics/.

Little, Graham Richard. "Deloitte Human Capital Trends in Perspective: The Science of Organization Design and Operation." SSRN Electronic Journal, 2017. https://doi.org/10.2139/ssrn.2937125.

Revesencio, Jonha "Why Happy Employees Are 12% More Productive." Fast Company. July 31, 2015. https://www.fastcompany.com/3048751/happy-employees-are-12-more-productive-at-work.

"Shape Culture." Deloitte Insights. Accessed May 19, 2020. https://www2.deloitte.com/us/en/insights/focus/human-capital-trends/2016/impact-of-culture-on-business-strategy.html?id=us:2el:3dc:dup3020:awa:cons:hct16.

CHAPTER 1:

"Intangible: Definition of Intangible by Lexico." Lexico Dictionaries. Accessed May 19, 2020. https://www.lexico.com/en/definition/intangible.

Kobulnicky, Ben. "Does Culture Really Eat Strategy?" Medium. Startup Grind, February 15, 2019. https://medium.com/startup-grind/does-culture-really-eat-strategy-a3172df58912.

Kreps, David M. 1990. "Corporate culture and economic theory." Pp. 90-143 in J.E. Alt and K.A. Shepsle (eds.). Perspectives on Positive Political Economy Cambridge, England: Cambridge University Press.

Little, Graham Richard. "Deloitte Human Capital Trends in Perspective: The Science of Organization Design and Operation." SSRN Electronic Journal, 2017. https://doi.org/10.2139/ssrn.2937125.

Merriam-Webster. s.v. "Culture." Accessed May 19, 2020. https://www.merriam-webster.com/dictionary/culture.

O'Reilly, Charles A. and Jennifer A. Chatman. 1996. "Culture as social control: corporations, culture and commitment." Research in Organizational Behavior 18: 157-200.

O'Reilly, Charles A. "Corporations, culture and commitment: Motivation and social control in organizations." California Management Review 31: 9-25. 1989.

Segal, Troy. "Corporate Bankruptcy: An Overview." Investopedia. Investopedia, May 15, 2020. https://www.investopedia.com/articles/01/120501.asp.

Segal, Troy. "Enron Scandal: The Fall of a Wall Street Darling." Investopedia. Investopedia, May 4, 2020. https://www.investopedia.com/updates/enron-scandal-summary/.

Sinek, Simon. *Start with Why: How Great Leaders Inspire Everyone to Take Action.* London: Portfolio Penguin, 2019.

Sorensen, Jesper. "Note on Organizational Culture." Stanford Graduate School of Business, 2009. https://www.gsb.stanford.edu/faculty-research/case-studies/note-organizational-culture.

Sorensen, Jesper B. 2002. "The strength of corporate culture and the reliability of firm performance." Administrative Science Quarterly 47: 70-91. Zucker, Lynne G. 1977.

Lexico Dictionaries. s.v. "Tangible: Definition of Tangible by Lexico." Accessed May 19, 2020. https://www.lexico.com/en/definition/tangible.

"The EntreLeadership Podcast." by Ken Coleman. Episode #132: "Todd Duncan—The New Rules of Customer Service." January 31, 2016. https://podcasts.apple.com/us/podcast/the-entreleadership-podcast/id435836905?i=1000361722096.

"ToddDuncan." Home. Accessed May 19, 2020. http://6000dol-laregg.com/.

"Trust Is the Result of Repeated Truth." Todd Duncan. Accessed May 19, 2020. http://toddduncan.com/.

CHAPTER 2:

"About Google, Our Culture & Company News." Google. Accessed May 20, 2020. https://about.google/?fg=1&utm_source=goo-gle-US&utm_medium=referral&utm_campaign=hp-header.

Brown, Brené. *Dare to Lead: Brave Work. Tough Conversations. Whole Hearts.* Random House Publishing Group. 2018

Groysberg, Boris, Jeremiah Lee, Jesse Price, and J. Yo-Jud Cheng. "The Leader's Guide to Corporate Culture: How to Manage the Eight Critical Elements of Organizational Life." Harvard Business School. January 1, 2018. https://www.hbs.edu/faculty/Pages/item.aspx?num=53726.

Katzenbach, Jon R., Ilona Steffen, and Caroline Kronley. "Cultural Change That Sticks."

Harvard Business Review, November 27, 2019. https://hbr.org/2012/07/cultural-change-that-sticks.

Pink, Daniel H. *Drive: The Surprising Truth About What Motivates Us.* Edinburgh: Canongate, 2011.

"Understanding the Pareto Principle (The 80/20 Rule)." BetterExplained. Accessed May 20, 2020. https://betterexplained.com/articles/understanding-the-pareto-principle-the-8020-rule/.

CHAPTER 3:

"18 Captivating Mission Statement Examples You Need to Read." Tampa Inbound Marketing Agency. Accessed May 20, 2020. https://www.bluleadz.com/blog/15-of-the-very-best-mission-statement-examples.

Brown, Tom. "Turning Mission Statements into Action." Harvard Business Review. September 1, 1997. https://store.hbr.org/product/turning-mission-statements-into-action/U9709B.

BusinessDictionary.com. s.v. "When Was the Last Time You Said This?" Accessed May 20, 2020. http://www.businessdictionary.com/definition/mission-statement.html.

O'Leary, John. "Inspirational Leadership." John O'Leary. April 6, 2020. http://johnolearyinspires.com/.

"The EntreLeadership Podcast" hosted by Ken Coleman. Episode #119: "John O'Leary-Living an Inspired Life." Ramsey Solutions. November 1, 2015. https://podcasts.apple.com/us/podcast/the-entreleadership-podcast/id435836905?i=1000356135862.

CHAPTER 4:

"18 Captivating Mission Statement Examples You Need to Read." Tampa Inbound Marketing Agency. Accessed May 20, 2020.

https://www.bluleadz.com/blog/15-of-the-very-best-mission-statement-examples.

Collins, Jim. Accessed May 20, 2020. https://www.jimcollins.com/.

Collins, Jim, and Jerry I. Porras. "Building Your Company's Vision." Harvard Business Review, January 19, 2016. https://hbr.org/1996/09/building-your-companys-vision.

Evans, Leonard. "Southwest Airlines Co.'s Mission Statement & Vision Statement (An Analysis)." Panmore Institute. May 30, 2019. http://panmore.com/southwest-airlines-vision-statement-mission-statement-analysis.

Jick, Todd D. "The Vision Thing." Harvard Business Review. September 26, 1989

Msa. "Nike Mission Statement 2020: Nike Mission & Vision Analysis." Mission Statement Academy. May 12, 2020. https://mission-statement.com/nike/.

Porras, Jerry I. Stanford Graduate School of Business. Accessed May 20, 2020. https://www.gsb.stanford.edu/faculty-research/faculty/jerry-i-porras.

Sinek, Simon. *Start with Why: How Great Leaders Get Everyone on the Same Page.* New York: Portfolio, 2009

"The EntreLeadership Podcast" hosted by Ken Coleman. Episode #130: "Jim Collins-How to Build an Enduring, Great Company." Ramsey Solutions. January 17, 2016. https://pod-

casts.apple.com/us/podcast/the-entreleadership-podcast/
id435836905?i=1000360879572.

CHAPTER 5:

Cockerell, Lee "About." November 12, 2018. https://www.leecock-
erell.com/about/. Collins, James C. *Good to Great: Why Some
Companies Make the Leap... and Others Don't.* New York, NY:
William Collins, 2001

Goleman, Daniel. "What Makes a Leader?" Harvard Business
Review, July 18, 2017. https://hbr.org/2004/01/what-makes-a-
leader.

"The EntreLeadership Podcast" by Ken Coleman. Episode #115:
"Creating Leadership Magic the Disney Way" Ramsey Solutions. October 4, 2015. https://podcasts.apple.com/us/podcast/
the-entreleadershippodcast/id435836905?i=1000354039415.

CHAPTER 6:

"Diversity and Inclusion Definitions." Diversity and Inclusion
Definitions—Ferris State University. Accessed May 20, 2020.
https://www.ferris.edu/htmls/administration/president/diver-
sityoffice/definitions.htm.

Janove, Jathan, and J.d. "Putting Humanity into HR Compliance:
Become Aware of Unconscious Bias." SHRM. August 16, 2019.
https://www.shrm.org/resourcesandtools/hr-topics/behav-
ioral-competencies/global-and-cultural-effectiveness/pages/
putting-humanity-into-hr-compliance-become-aware-of-un-
conscious-bias.aspx.

Johnson, Kate. *Pull Yourself Together: Owning Your Difference to Get Ahead*. New Degree Press. 2019

Krentz, Matt. "Survey: What Diversity and Inclusion Policies Do Employees Actually Want?"

Harvard Business Review, February 5, 2019. https://hbr.org/2019/02/survey-what-diversity-and-inclusion-policies-do-employees-actually-want.

Miller, Stephen. "JPMorgan Chase Settles Paternity Leave Suit over 'Primary Caregiver' for $5 Million." SHRM. August 16, 2019. https://www.shrm.org/resourcesandtools/hr-topics/benefits/pages/jpmorgan-chase-settles-paternity-suit-over-primary-caregiver-leave.aspx.

Poston, Dudley and Rogelio Sáenz. "US Will Be 'Majority-Minority' in next 25 Years." UPI. April 30, 2019. https://www.upi.com/Top_News/Voices/2019/04/30/US-will-be-majority-minority-in-next-25-years/2971556626784/.

Somen, Mondal. "Diversity and Inclusion: A Beginner's Guide for HR Professionals." Ideal. May 4, 2020. https://ideal.com/diversity-and-inclusion/.

II, Vann R. Newkirk. "How the Myth of Reverse Racism Drives the Affirmative Action Debate." The Atlantic. Atlantic Media Company, August 10, 2017. https://www.theatlantic.com/education/archive/2017/08/myth-of-reverse-racism/535689/.

CHAPTER 7:

Adkins, Amy. "Only 35% of US Managers Are Engaged in Their Jobs." Gallup.com. May 14, 2020. https://www.gallup.com/workplace/236552/managers-engaged-jobs.aspx.

Lencioni, Patrick: "The Table Group." Accessed May 22, 2020. https://www.tablegroup.com/pat/#pat.

Lencioni, Patrick. *The Truth About Employee Engagement: A Fable About Addressing the Three Root Causes of Job Misery.* San Francisco, CA: Jossey-Bass & Pfeiffer, 2016.

Novak, David. David Novak Leadership. Accessed May 22, 2020. https://davidnovakleadership.com/novak-david/.

Rogers, Kristie. "Do Your Employees Feel Respected?" Harvard Business Review, June 21, 2018. https://hbr.org/2018/07/do-your-employees-feel-respected.

Schwantes, Marcel. "The Surprising Reason Why So Many Employees Quit Within the First 6 Months." Inc.com. July 25, 2019. https://www.inc.com/marcel-schwantes/surprising-reason-why-employees-quit.html.

Snyder, Benjamin. "Half Of Us Have Quit Our Job Because of a Bad Boss." Fortune. April 2, 2015. https://fortune.com/2015/04/02/quit-reasons/.

"10 Easy Ways to Recognize Your Team." EntreLeadership, December 10, 2017. https://www.entreleadership.com/blog/10-easy-ways-recognize-team.

"The EntreLeadership Podcast" hosted by Ken Coleman. Ramsey Solutions. Episode #188: "David Novak-Why Recognition Matters." February 26, 2017. https://podcasts.apple.com/us/podcast/the-entreleadership-podcast/id435836905?i=1000381931043.

Total Solutions. Accessed May 22, 2020. https://www.totalrsolutions.com/employee-incentive-plan-closer-look-goal-setting-success/.

CHAPTER 8:

Noe, Raymond A. *Employee Training & Development*. McGraw-Hill Higher Education. 7th editioned. 2016.

"The Entreleadership Podcast" Hosted by Ken Coleman. Ramsey Solutions. Episode #96: "Tom Ziglar-The Keys to Top Performance." Accessed May 22, 2020 https://www.entreleadership.com/blog/podcasts/tom-ziglar-top-performance.

"The Michigan State University Talent Management & Development Course Materials." Talent Management & Development. Accessed May 22, 2020

"The 70-20-10 Model for Learning and Development." Training Industry, January 28, 2014. https://trainingindustry.com/wiki/content-development/the-702010-model-for-learning-and-development/.

CHAPTER 9:

"Leaders Eat Last." Simon Sinek. Accessed May 25, 2020. https://simonsinek.com/product/leaders-eat-last/?ref=home.

Sinek, Simon. *Leaders Eat Last*. Portfolio; Reprint, Revised Edition, 2014. Kindle.

"The Entreleadership Podcast" hosted by Ken Coleman. Ramsey Solutions. Episode #75: "Simon Sinek-Why Leaders Eat Last." Accessed May 25, 2020. https://www.entreleadership.com/blog/podcasts/simon-sinek-leaders-eat-last.

CHAPTER 10:

Brown, Brené. *Dare to Lead: Brave Work. Tough Conversations. Whole Hearts*. Random House Publishing Group, 2018

Willink, Jocko, and Leif Babin. *Extreme Ownership: How US Navy SEALs Lead and Win*. St. Martin's Press; First Edition, 2015

CONCLUSION: FULL CIRCLE

Harter, Jim, and Annamarie Mann. "The Right Culture: Not Just About Employee Satisfaction." Gallup.com. Gallup. May 5, 2020

Land O'Lakes. Accessed May 25, 2020. http://www.makingafortune.biz/list-of-companies-l/land-o-lakes.htm.